# PRIOR LEARNING PORTFOLIOS

## A Representative Collection

WITHDRAW

**DENISE M. HART**

Fairleigh Dickinson University

**JERRY H. HICKERSON**

Winston-Salem State University

CAEL

KENDALLHUNT
PROFESSIONAL

Cover image sources:
  Men with hard hats © Dmitriy Shironosov, 2008
  Doctor with colleague © János Gehring, 2008
  Woman on computer © Monkey Business Images, 2008
  All used under license from Shutterstock, Inc.

Copyright © 2009 by the Council for Adult and Experiential Learning

ISBN 978-0-7575-5887-0

Kendall/Hunt Publishing Company has the exclusive rights to reproduce this work,
to prepare derivative works from this work, to publicly distribute this work,
to publicly perform this work and to publicly display this work.

All rights reserved. No part of this publication may be reproduced,
stored in a retrieval system, or transmitted, in any form or by any
means, electronic, mechanical, photocopying, recording, or otherwise,
without the prior written permission of the copyright owner.

Printed in the United States of America
10  9  8  7  6  5  4  3  2  1

*For my parents, with love.*

D.M.H

*For Heather, Darren, Brian, and Shannon.*

J.H.H.

# CONTENTS

*Acknowledgments* . . . . . . . . . . . . . . . . . . . . . . . . . . . . . . . . . . . . . . . . . . . . . . . . .vii

*How to Use This Book* . . . . . . . . . . . . . . . . . . . . . . . . . . . . . . . . . . . . . . . . . . . . .ix

*Introduction* . . . . . . . . . . . . . . . . . . . . . . . . . . . . . . . . . . . . . . . . . . . . . . . . . . . . .xi

**CHAPTER 1**   THIRTY-FIVE YEARS OF PLA: WE'VE COME A LONG WAY . . . . . . . . . . . . .1

**CHAPTER 2**   PRIOR LEARNING ASSESSMENT TODAY: STATES OF THE ART . . . . . . . . . .11

**CHAPTER 3**   THE TEN STANDARDS FOR ASSESSING LEARNING . . . . . . . . . . . . . . .17

**CHAPTER 4**   IDENTIFYING ASSESSMENT APPROACHES TO MATCH
THE NEEDS OF THE STUDENT . . . . . . . . . . . . . . . . . . . . . . . . . . . . .21

**CHAPTER 5**   ASHFORD UNIVERSITY . . . . . . . . . . . . . . . . . . . . . . . . . . . . . . . . . .25

**CHAPTER 6**   ATHABASCA UNIVERSITY . . . . . . . . . . . . . . . . . . . . . . . . . . . . . . . .33

**CHAPTER 7**   CHARTER OAK STATE COLLEGE . . . . . . . . . . . . . . . . . . . . . . . . . . .39

**CHAPTER 8**   EMPIRE STATE COLLEGE . . . . . . . . . . . . . . . . . . . . . . . . . . . . . . . .45

**CHAPTER 9**   REGIS UNIVERSITY . . . . . . . . . . . . . . . . . . . . . . . . . . . . . . . . . . . .53

**CHAPTER 10**   SPRING ARBOR UNIVERSITY . . . . . . . . . . . . . . . . . . . . . . . . . . . . .59

**CHAPTER 11**   ST. EDWARD'S UNIVERSITY . . . . . . . . . . . . . . . . . . . . . . . . . . . . .67

**CHAPTER 12**   ST. JOSEPH'S COLLEGE . . . . . . . . . . . . . . . . . . . . . . . . . . . . . . . .73

CHAPTER 13    VALDOSTA STATE UNIVERSITY . . . . . . . . . . . . . . . . . . . . . . . . . . . . . . . . . . .79

CHAPTER 14    VERMONT STATE COLLEGES . . . . . . . . . . . . . . . . . . . . . . . . . . . . . . . . . . . .85

CHAPTER 15    THE UNIVERSITY OF ALABAMA, EXTERNAL DEGREE PROGRAM . . . . . . . . . . . . . .91

APPENDIX A    CONTRIBUTORS AND AFFILIATIONS . . . . . . . . . . . . . . . . . . . . . . . . . . . . . . .101

APPENDIX B    TERMS AND ABBREVIATIONS ASSOCIATED WITH
              PRIOR LEARNING ASSESSMENT . . . . . . . . . . . . . . . . . . . . . . . . . . . . . . . . .103

              REFERENCES . . . . . . . . . . . . . . . . . . . . . . . . . . . . . . . . . . . . . . . . . . . . .111

              INDEX . . . . . . . . . . . . . . . . . . . . . . . . . . . . . . . . . . . . . . . . . . . . . . . . . .119

              CD:  SAMPLE PORTFOLIOS AND RELATED DOCUMENTS

              Ashford University

              Athabasca University

              Charter Oak State College

              Empire State College

              Regis University

              Spring Arbor University

              St. Edward's University

              St. Joseph's College

              Valdosta State University

              Vermont State Colleges

              The University of Alabama, External Degree Program

# ACKNOWLEDGMENTS

To our colleagues, students, friends and family for their insights and support, thank you. And thanks specifically, to Dennis and Karen for their patience and prodding.

Thanks to Cynthia Kasee, Ph.D., of Winston-Salem State University for her editorial assistance on select chapters and Craig M. Cannon, B.A., of Fairleigh Dickinson University, Graphic Designer, for his expertise in creating consistency in the entire printed text, uniformity of all documents and the production of the accompanying CD-ROM.

Of course, we extend much gratitude to our contributors for sharing their portfolio models and/or conceptual ideas surrounding portfolio assessment as a tool for the evaluation of experiential learning, making this text a reality.

Our best to the many future prior learning assessment practitioners, for whom we hope to open new doors, new perceptions, and new practices in experiential learning.

Denise M. Hart

Jerry H. Hickerson

# HOW TO USE THIS BOOK

In utilizing this text, you may identify portfolio samples that match those you'd like to develop for yourself as a student, for your institution as a Prior Learning Assessment Planning Group, and/or merely of interest to preview diverse models of portfolio assessment that are currently practiced and globally representative. The purpose of this text is to provide *samples* not *exemplars*.

The chapters within the text itself elucidate the policies and procedures for review of each institution's portfolio sample (located on the CD-ROM). It is recommended that you read the chapter either concurrently with review of the portfolio sample or review the portfolio sample subsequent to having read the chapter. In this way, you will understand the institution's expectations for those who participate in the portfolio assessment process.

The text is not meant to be read from "front to back" but rather selecting those chapters that are of most interest to you. As you examine all of the chapters, you will find similarities and differences within a standardized, valid, and reliable framework.

The materials provided by the contributors include more than just examples of portfolios models; they include handbooks, guidelines, flow charts, information about the location of portfolio assessment in the context of a degree, through and including a statistical profile of the institutions' students who participated in prior learning assessment during the academic year 2006–2007. All information was current at the time of collection of data and the publication of this text. Obviously, data change for any academic year, including the numbers of students who participate in portfolio assessment at any given institution, the associated fees and/or compensation of evaluators, etc. Thus, the reader may want to check the website of the institutions (listed in Appendix A) for current statistics.

The CD-ROM that accompanies the text contains all documents provided by the contributing institutions, including their portfolio sample(s) [some of which are hypothetical] and relevant materials. Additionally, you shall find the number of credits requested, number of credits awarded and means of transcription for the various portfolio samples included. Restrain from looking at the Assessment Outcomes item for each institution until you have had sufficient opportunity to study the documents.

Upon review of both the text and CD-ROM, consider the following:

1.  Evaluate the portfolio sample(s). If this individual were to present the document to your institution: Would the content be appropriate? How would the content be handled? That is, which department would be responsible for the review? Would the portfolio document(s) yield credit? As a student, does this look like your experiential learning portfolio?

2. Using the supporting materials from the associated institutions: Does the portfolio sample "fit" within the context of the policies and procedures for portfolio review at your institution? If necessary, how would you modify the portfolio sample and related documentation for your institution and review process?

3. Using the supporting materials from the associated institutions: Are there sufficient, accurate, authentic, and relevant artifacts to accompany the portfolio sample? As a student, can you glean ideas about primary and secondary evidence to accompany your own portfolio?

4. What did you like about the portfolio sample(s) and related materials? What might you change? Why?

Remember that learning is a journey, though not everyone takes the same road.

Good luck! . . . ¡Buena suerte! . . . Bonne Chance!

# INTRODUCTION

"The word portfolio came into English from Italian in the early eighteenth century. The original was portafoglio, something in which one carried sheets of paper. And this was its first meaning in English: a receptacle or case in which to carry loose papers, prints, drawings and the like, a meaning it still has. Much later it was applied to the set of one's investments, no doubt seen as a collection of bits of valuable paper (Quinion, 1998 as cited in Trent & Chen, 2008, para. 4)." Today, the portfolio has also come to mean a method or tool by which one might demonstrate an expanse of learning.

Assessment via portfolio is most often used by the nontraditional adult learner who can display experiential learning gained from jobs, travel, community service, and leisure activities to name a few sources. To be considered credit-worthy, the knowledge and skills gained through experiential learning would generally go beyond the range of abilities of the average, traditional student. Consequently, adults form the cohort who are drawn to institutions that feature Prior Learning Assessment. Why is this important to the academy? As reported by Robert A. Sevier, in his presentation at the National Association of Independent Colleges and Universities' Conference (February, 2008, slide 37), "40 percent of college students are aged 25 or older; 58 percent are aged 22 or older, with only 16 percent of students who [actually] fit the traditional model: age 18–22 years old, attending college full-time, and living on-campus (see also Stokes, 2006 as cited in Harms, 2008). Sevier also predicted that (t)here are six growth markets in higher education:

1. Students of color
2. Adult students, including seniors
3. Commuter students
4. Part-time students
5. Women (of almost all ages)
6. International students together

[and that] the market for full-time residential students is declining and will continue to decline for at least a generation (2008, slide 12). These adult students are particularly interested in flexibility, convenience, credit for [learning from] life experience, accelerated completion, valid learning experience[s], and multiple learning alternatives (2008, slide 39)." In the paper, Serving Adult Students: What Really Matters? The "Must Do" List for Colleges and Universities (Harms, 2008), the researchers found, [that] the issue of experiential learning credit is a significant factor in the college-selection process. For those potential students who were likely to return for a bachelor's degree, 75 percent reported that they were much more interested in institutions that provided credit for their [learning from] life experience. At the graduate level, this percentage slips to 56 percent, but is still a factor" (p. 4). Thus, the need for a valid, reliable, means of measurement and evaluation is important to the learner.

In both Council for Adult and Experiential Learning (CAEL) Executive Summaries, *Serving Adult Learners in Higher Education, Findings from CAEL's Benchmarking Study* and *Serving Adult Learners in Adult Education, Principles of Effectiveness*, (CAEL, 1999 & 2000), it is demonstrated that assessment of prior experiential learning is a key to becoming an Adult Learner Focused Institution.

The present text is born from a need to provide portfolio program models that demonstrate institutional practices of experiential learning.

We present in this work—institutional policies and procedures, sample portfolios from eleven different institutions, and related contributed documents. The portfolios provided are recent but, beyond that, the differences among the institutions are many:

◆ **EXPERIENCE.** The established portfolio assessment programs in this text represent a timeframe ranging from the 1970's to the current year, 2008.

◆ **"PUBLIC" INSTITUTIONS.** The six publicly supported colleges and universities include the following: a distance learning institution in Canada with a global mission; two solely adult focused (versus traditional) universities; a state-wide program begun in the 1970's that manages the assessment of prior learning through numerous two- and four-year colleges; an external degree program begun in the 1970's at a flagship university; and a state university just beginning its PLA program.

◆ **"PRIVATE" INSTITUTIONS.** Privately supported colleges include three affiliated with the Roman Catholic Church, one with the Free Methodist Church, and one proprietary university.

◆ **REGIONAL ACCREDITATION.** All eleven institutions are accredited by their respective associations of colleges and schools—three by North Central, three by the Southern Association, two by New England, and three by Middle States—including Athabasca University with degree-granting authority by the Province of Alberta as well.

While approaches to portfolio assessment may be different, there are also consistencies, particularly as related to standards. You will find many of them in the representative Sample Portfolios. We have also enlisted colleagues to share essential and significant information in early chapters about the history of PLA, the present status of PLA in various states, standards and the guidance of students through the PLA process from initial advisement to the credit placed on the transcript by the registrar. Primary contacts and additional contributors (and their affiliations) to the text, found in Appendix A, worked with the authors to provide the substance of the chapters in print and on the disk.

Through this edition, we trust that persons interested in adult education will reach a greater understanding of the variety of approaches to Prior Learning Assessment being used by various colleges and universities—demonstrating the cross-section of practices established from decades of research, theory and practice. These are frameworks for evaluation which fulfill the mission of each institution selected to participate in this endeavor. They should not, therefore, be considered model portfolios for any other institution but, rather, portfolio models from which ideas may come to contribute to a portfolio program in the process of development or to the debate about what is the best way to assess learning through a portfolio.

# THIRTY-FIVE YEARS OF PLA

## WE'VE COME A LONG WAY

Diana Bamford-Rees
Council for Adult and Experiential Learning

Since 1974, the Council for Adult and Experiential Learning (CAEL) has worked with accrediting bodies, employers, and education organizations to develop a common language and foundation for assessing prior learning. CAEL took the lead in articulating the philosophical basis for prior learning assessment (PLA), as well as in developing policies and procedures for implementation in an academically sound manner. CAEL has published a wide array of information including standards of quality assurance, guidelines for implementing portfolio PLA, sample portfolios, and institutional PLA research. In addition, CAEL has sponsored many events to disseminate information related to prior learning, has developed networks among institutions interested in prior learning, and has trained administrators and faculty in the procedures of PLA.

There are, perhaps, as many ways to define and assess prior learning as there are institutions. Generally, PLA refers to an assessment of knowledge or skills attained prior to, or outside of enrollment, at a postsecondary institution, for the purpose of awarding college credit. The history of PLA dates back as early as World War II when the American Council on Education (ACE) began assessing knowledge and skills gained in the military. This initial assessment was followed by formalized testing in the mid-1960s and the assessment movement led by CAEL, which began in the mid-1970s.

## ADULT LEARNERS AND HIGHER EDUCATION IN THE 1970S

Part-time study, intermittent enrollment, and open admissions became more common in the 1970s, especially in struggling private colleges and regional state institutions that were beginning to experience a decline in the traditional college population. The ability to meet enrollment quotas with adults meant survival for some of these colleges and, therefore, many institutions developed new programs in response to the needs of the adult learners. These programs came to be known as "non-traditional" programs.

The pressure from legislatures and the public on higher education to become more accountable for its performance led to a variety of new approaches to assess what students learned, emphasizing what was learned rather than what was taught. It did not take much to demonstrate that a number of students already knew what colleges and universities wanted to teach, and that the college degree could be "time-shortened" (Carnegie Commission on Higher Education, 1971).

This benefited adult students. If adult students felt they had already met some college requirements, they could request an assessment by a variety of new methods. These included standardized tests such as the College-Level Examination Program (CLEP), which the College Board had begun administering in 1967, and homegrown examinations (challenge exams) designed by faculty members to test adult students' knowledge of material to be covered by various department courses. If adult students had served in the military, they could take examinations through the United States Armed Services Institute and possibly receive academic credit for courses taken in the military through the Office on Educational Credits and Credentials of the American Council on Education (ACE), operating since 1945. As a result of adaptations of assessment techniques developed for industry, adults could take performance tests, engage in simulations, be observed in action, submit to interviews, or could present portfolios for academic credit.

In the early 1970s, a number of new institutions, with the primary mission of serving adult learners, were born. Among these were the Community College of Vermont (1970); Empire State College, New York (1971); Minnesota Metropolitan State College (1971); New College, University of Alabama (1971); Thomas A. Edison State College, New Jersey (1972); Florida International University (1972); and The College of Public and Community Service at the University of Massachusetts—Boston (1972). These institutions, plus a few dozen other colleges and universities that realized that learning gained through work and life experiences is often comparable to learning gained through traditional classroom education, were the early pioneers of PLA.

## SOME DEFINITIONS

*Prior learning* is a term used by educators to describe learning that a person acquires outside of a traditional academic environment and before college enrollment. This learning may have been acquired through work experience, employer training programs, independent study, non-credit courses, volunteer or community service, travel, or non-college courses or seminars.

*Prior learning assessment* (*PLA*) or *assessment of prior learning* (*APL*) are terms used by colleges to describe the process by which an individual's experiential learning is assessed and evaluated for purposes of granting credit, certification, or advanced standing toward further education or training. There are four generally accepted approaches to PLA and, when properly conducted, all ensure academic quality: (1) National standardized exams in specified disciplines, e.g., AP exams, CLEP tests, Excelsior college exams, DSST exams; (2) challenge exams for local courses; (3) evaluated non-college programs, e.g., ACE evaluations of corporate training and military training; and (4) individualized assessments. It is this fourth category—individualized assessments—to which the portfolio assessment method, the focus of this book, belongs.

In the PLA world, the term *portfolio* is used to describe a collection of evidence in support of a person's claim for credit through a prior learning assessment process. It is a formal communication presented by the student to the college as a petition process requesting credit or recognition for learning outside the college classroom. Through the portfolio, the student makes his/her case by identifying learning achievements clearly and succinctly, and by providing sufficient supporting information and documentation so that faculty can use it, alone or in combination with other evidence, as the basis for their evaluations.

## CAEL, ETS, AND EARLY RESEARCH ON PLA METHODS

With funding from the Carnegie Corporation and the Education Foundation of America, the prestigious Commission on Non-Traditional Study was founded in 1971 under the joint sponsorship of Educational Testing Service (ETS) and the College Board. This Commission would study the current status, assess needs, and recommend directions for the future of non-traditional education. Among its fifty-seven recommendations, two laid the groundwork for what would become CAEL. These recommendations were:

◆ New devices and techniques should be perfected to measure the outcomes of many types of non-traditional study and to assess the educative effect of work experience and community service.

◆ Systems of quality control should be built into the instruction and evaluative aspects of non-traditional study whenever possible.

Alden Dunham, the officer at Carnegie who had backed the Commission, suggested that more guidance was needed for the development of the "new devices and techniques." Perhaps in response to the Commission, non-traditional programs were applying to the Carnegie Corporation for support. Dunham, therefore, thought a joint effort would make more sense than funding a series of individual projects. After several preliminary meetings (late in 1973) to talk about how to tackle the validation of non-traditional education, ETS and ten task force institutions [Antioch College (now University); Community College of Vermont; El Paso Community College; Empire State College; Florida International University; Framingham State College; Minnesota Metropolitan State College (now Metropolitan State University); New College, University of Alabama; San Francisco State College (now University); and Thomas A. Edison College] submitted a joint proposal to the

Carnegie Corporation for a three-year research project. The project was funded in the spring of 1974 and named the Cooperative Assessment of Experiential Learning (CAEL) project.

## CAEL I: A Project in Assessment

The research question to be answered was: "Is it possible to assess, validly and reliably, learning acquired outside the classroom for the award of college credit?"

The CAEL project was a project in assessment with primary and secondary goals:

- ◆ **Primary Goal:** To identify, and make more widely known, the best practices in assessment of experiential learning.

- ◆ **Secondary Goal:** To devise and develop other, and better, effective assessment processes.

The project placed emphasis on the following four points:

1. Assessment of the achievement of interpersonal skills
2. Use of portfolios in assessment of prior learning
3. Assessment of learning outcomes of work experience
4. Use of expert judgment in assessing learning outcomes

During the three-year period (1974–1977), the CAEL project enrolled 270 institutions as fee-paying members, conducted twelve operational (implementation) model programs, trained twelve institutional teams of faculty assessors, conducted six national conferences (referred to as "Assemblies") to disseminate the research among members, and released more than fifty working papers and reports and twenty-seven publications. One of these publications was Warren Willingham's *Principles of Good Practice in Experiential Learning*, which set forth the ten principles for quality assurance in the assessment of experiential learning.

At the conclusion of the CAEL I project, the answer to the question about whether it was possible to conduct valid and reliable assessment of learning gained from work or life experience was yes, with the proviso that appropriate procedures and processes for evaluating that learning were in place.

## CAEL II: More Research, New Publications and a Lot of Training

At the spring 1976 CAEL Assembly, the members agreed overwhelmingly to CAEL's continuation as an independent organization. A decision was made to keep the CAEL acronym but to change two of the words: from "Cooperative" to "Council" and from "Assessment" to "Advancement." The Steering Committee was reconstituted as a Board of Trustees, and Morris Keeton, previously the Chair of the Steering Committee, became the Executive Director of the newly incorporated 501(c)(3)—CAEL II.

Keeton proposed these priorities for CAEL II: that it (1) improve the assessment of learning outcomes, (2) promote wider use of mixes of experiential and theoretical learning in classroom and non-classroom settings, and (3) become a "non-lobbying advocate" among learners, educators, administrators, and policy makers. Additional priorities for the new CAEL were to: (1) develop methods and materials for faculty development and training for administrators in the assessment of experiential learning, and (2) work with the accrediting associations for acceptance and endorsement of PLA practices.

The faculty and administrator training priority was greatly advanced by a generous grant from the W. K. Kellogg Foundation to support the CAEL Institutional Development Program (IDP). IDP extended many of the techniques pioneered by the original CAEL, especially the Faculty Development Program. A total of 461 institutions participated in this three-year (1977 to 1980) program. The program received additional funding, and by 1983 IDP had underwritten over 80,000 PLA training days for higher education faculty and staff throughout the United States.

Prior Learning Assessment achieved another milestone in 1979 when, as a result of CAEL's work with the accrediting bodies and other key national higher education associations, the American Association of Collegiate Registrars and Admissions Officers (AACRAO), the American Council on Education (ACE), and the Council for Higher Education Accreditation issued a joint statement endorsing PLA and the CAEL principles. This statement was reissued in 2001.

CAEL continued to publish in the fields of Experiential Learning and PLA. Between 1978 and 1982, Morris Keeton and Pamela Tate edited twenty Jossey-Bass *New Directions for Experiential Learning* sourcebooks. In 1982, Susan Rydell edited a collection of sample portfolios which CAEL published in a volume entitled *Creditable Portfolios: Dimensions in Diversity.* And, in 1985, CAEL published the first edition of a student guide entitled *Earn College Credit for What You Know.* The text provided information for students on how to prepare a portfolio for assessment of their prior learning.

## PLA IN THE 1980s

Prior learning assessment, especially portfolio assessment, was growing rapidly due to the combination of many forces that brought adults into higher education during the late 1970s: the efforts of CAEL and other organizations to legitimize learning throughout life, a restructuring in the U.S. economy requiring that workers be trained for new jobs, the entry of vast numbers of women into the job market, and the need on the part of many colleges and universities to attract adults to offset declines in the traditional college-age population. With more adult students came more pressure to recognize what they had already learned.

By the early 1980s, the assessment and crediting of prior learning had expanded greatly. In 1974, the original CAEL project had located just over forty PLA programs. Four years later, a survey identified a total of 211, of which 143 used portfolio assessment. In 1980, the Office on Educational Credit and Credentials at ACE sent out a questionnaire to learn how colleges and universities were handling extra-institutional learning. Almost all of the more than 2,000 institutions that responded awarded experiential learning credit, most commonly by examination. *Almost 1,100 said they had portfolio programs for PLA.*

In a survey commissioned by CAEL for the external evaluation of the Kellogg-funded IDP, the American College Testing (ACT) Program estimated that about 1.2 million quarter hours of college credit were awarded for prior learning during 1980–1981; in contrast, only approximately 690,000 quarter hour credits in 1973–1974. About twelve percent of the credits awarded in 1973–1974 were based on portfolios and other individualized approaches; by 1980–1981, this changed to thirty-one percent. Adults using individualized assessment of prior learning increased from some 4,000 in 1974 to more than 30,000 in 1981.

In 1989, CAEL published Urban Whitaker's *Assessing Learning: Standards, Principles, & Procedures.* This book expanded, and replaced, Willingham's 1977 publication *Principles of Good Practice in Assessing Experiential Learning,* which set forth principles for quality assurance in assessment of learning. The Willingham book had long been "the Bible of prior learning assessment"; throughout the 1990s and into the twenty-first century, PLA practitioners transferred the name to the Whitaker text, dubbing it the "PLA Bible." The Whitaker book outlines the ten principles of good practice and standards of excellence—both academic and administrative—in the assessment of learning. Adopted in whole or in part by several regional accrediting bodies, the CAEL "Ten Standards for Quality Assurance" are internationally recognized as the best way to ensure that reliability and quality are maintained while real learning is appropriately recognized.

## WHAT NATIONAL SURVEYS TELL US ABOUT PLA

Throughout the years, CAEL has conducted national surveys to determine institutional practices with regard to PLA. These surveys are sent to all regionally accredited colleges and universities in the United States. The 1981 survey conducted by CAEL and published as a five-volume set of regional directories, found that 530 institutions had PLA portfolio programs. Another survey in 1984 identified 552 schools with portfolio assessment programs.

CAEL's 1991 National PLA Survey was sent to 3,694 institutions; 1,736 (47 percent) responded and 50 percent of these reported the use of portfolio assessment. The results of this survey were published in *Prior Learning Assessment: Results of a Nationwide Institutional Survey* (Fugate and Chapman, 1992).

In 1996, a national survey of institutional PLA practices was sent to 2,421 institutions with responses from 1,135 (also a 47 percent response rate). Of the respondents, 55 percent reported use of portfolio assessment. The results of this survey were published in *Prior Learning Assessment: A Guidebook to American Institutional Practices* (Zucker, Johnson, and Flint, 1999).

A summary of the results of CAEL's most recent PLA survey conducted in 2006 is published in *Prior Learning Assessment at Home and Abroad* (Excerpts from the CAEL Forum and News, November 2007). These responses show that most institutions accept PLA methods such as CLEP exams (85 percent) and AP exams (84 percent), similar to the acceptance patterns from the national PLA surveys conducted in 1991 and 1996. The use of portfolio assessment is becoming more common (66 percent in 2006 compared with 55 percent in 1996 and 50 percent in 1991.) Portfolio assessment is the single PLA method that has increased in use in the past decade.

## Comparisons of 1991, 1996, and 2006 CAEL National PLA Survey Data: PLA Methods Accepted

|  | 1991 | 1996 | 2006 |
|---|---|---|---|
| CLEP Exams | 88% | 87% | 85% |
| AP Exams | 90% | 92% | 84% |
| Excelsior Exams | 35% | 27% | 27% |
| DSST Exams | 52% | 62% | 48% |
| Challenge Exams | 72% | 72% | 57% |
| ACE Guides—Credit Recommendations | 75% | 78% | 70% |
| PORTFOLIO ASSESSMENT | 50% | 55% | 66% |

## PLA RESOURCES AND TRAINING OPPORTUNITIES

CAEL publishes books to support and advance the practice of quality assessment of prior learning. In 2006, new editions of *Earn College Credit for What You Know* (Colvin, 4th ed.) and *Assessing Learning: Standards, Principles & Procedures* (Fiddler, Marienau, and Whitaker, 2nd ed.) were released. This long-awaited text and CD-ROM of student portfolios, "Prior Learning Portfolios: A Representative Collection" (Hart and Hickerson), will be an important addition to the collection of PLA literature.

Each November, CAEL hosts an international conference that provides an opportunity for individuals from education, government, labor, and business concerned with adult learning issues to come together to learn from nationally known experts and to participate in workshops, roundtable discussions, special interest groups, and networking sessions. Many of the conference sessions and pre-conference training events focus on prior learning assessment.

CAEL offers several classroom-based PLA workshops to support and train PLA practitioners. *PLA 101* is a "nuts and bolts" workshop on how to design and implement PLA programs that are consistent with high academic standards. The *Defining College-Level Learning* workshop takes participants beyond the basics; they learn how to use best practices in PLA and to explore the meaning of college-level learning from theoretical and practical perspectives. In the *Advising Adult Learners* workshop, participants learn to respond to the needs of adult learners and receive a toolkit of resources for advisors and students. These workshops are offered prior to the international conference in November and again at various locations around the country each spring. Arrangements can also be made for CAEL workshops to be delivered on-site at colleges or universities.

On-site PLA consulting to help colleges and universities develop effective, customized PLA programs is available through CAEL. These consultations are tailored to institution-specific prior learning issues.

In partnership with DePaul University, CAEL launched an on-line PLA Certification Program in 2000. The program consists of four web-based workshops each with four to seven modules. During each four-week workshop, participants progress through a series of structured activities that employ on-line and off-line materials. Each group of participants is assigned an on-line consultant to facilitate learning and provide feedback. Participants may discuss issues and activities within their learning group. Completion of the first two workshops leads to a Certificate of Professional Achievement as a Prior Learning Assessor. Participants who successfully complete all four facilitated workshops will be granted a Certificate of Mastery in Prior Learning Assessment.

## PLA ABROAD

Prior Learning Assessment is not limited to institutions in the United States. In his book, *Experiential Learning Around the World* published in 2000, Norman Evans cites examples of programs in nine countries: England, United States, Canada, France, Scotland, Ireland, Australia, New Zealand, and South Africa. In England, the process is referred to as APEL or APL (Assessment of Prior Experiential Learning or Assessment of Prior Learning). Canadians speak of PLAR (Prior Learning Assessment and Recognition) while the South Africans use the term RPL (Recognition of Prior Learning). All utilize some form of portfolio assessment.

## BEYOND THE FIRST THIRTY-FIVE YEARS

We have indeed come a long way in the development and refinement of PLA policies and methods. In thirty-five years, PLA has progressed through infancy, childhood, and the teen years into adulthood and it seems a reasonably safe assumption that PLA is here to stay.

I join the authors of this text, and other CAEL colleagues, in stating, with great enthusiasm, that we believe this book and the accompanying CD-ROM will be an invaluable tool for PLA practitioners. We wish you only the very best as you work with your learners to help them to receive the recognition they deserve for their prior learning.

N.B. The origin for the text and figures cited here are vast and inclusive of personal communications and multiple sources. Those listed in the references for this chapter provide the focal point for further research and avoid merely a chapter of citations.

# Timeline: Thirty-Five Years of Prior Learning Assessment: 1973 to 2008

| Year | Activity/Event |
|---|---|
| 1973 (and earlier) | ◆ Commission on Non-Traditional Study<br>◆ Office of External Degree Programs (ETS)<br>◆ Preliminary meeting of Carnegie Corporation/ETS to discuss need for standardized process to assess nonclassroom learning |
| 1974 | ◆ Ten task force institutions* and ETS launch CAEL Project (CAEL I) with Carnegie funding (March)<br>◆ Field research begins—54 institutions<br>◆ 182 Institutions join CAEL in the first year<br>◆ First CAEL NationalConference to disseminate early research findings (214 attendees) |
| 1974 to 1977 | ◆ ETS-based CAEL Project (CAEL I)<br>◆ Produced 27 publications (handbooks and guides for students and faculty, annotated bibliographies, *Principles of Good Practice in Experiential Learning* (Willingham) and 50+ working papers, institutional reports, and special project reports<br>◆ Conducted 6 national conferences to disseminate research findings among the members<br>◆ Conducted operational (implementation) models research (12 institutions)<br>◆ Conducted Faculty Development Program (12 institutions)<br>◆ 270 institutional members at end of CAEL I |
| 1977 | ◆ CAEL II operates independently of ETS<br>◆ Incorporates as 501(c)(3) and relocates to Maryland with Morris Keeton as Executive Director |
| 1979 | ◆ American Association of Collegiate Registrars and Admissions Officers (AACRAO), American Council on Education (ACE), and Council for Higher Education Accreditation endorse PLA and CAEL principles |
| 1978 | ◆ Kellogg-funded Institutional Development Program (IDP) launched by CAEL |
| 1981 | ◆ National PLA Survey conducted by CAEL resulting in the publication of *Wherever You Learned It: A Directory of Opportunities for Educational Credit* (McIntyre)—five regional volumes containing data from 530 institutions that had portfolio programs |
| 1982 | ◆ A collection of institutional models of student portfolios—*Creditable Portfolios: Dimensions in Diversity* (Rydell) published by CAEL |
| 1984 | ◆ National PLA Survey conducted by CAEL; 1,493 institutions responded—552 (37 percent) indicated use of portfolio assessment method |
| 1985 | ◆ First edition of *Earn College Credit for What You Know* (Simosko) published by CAEL |
| 1989 | ◆ First edition of *Assessing Learning: Standards, Principles & Procedures* (Whitaker) published by CAEL |

*(continues)*

# Timeline: Thirty-Five Years of Prior Learning Assessment: 1973 to 2008 *(continued)*

| Year | Activity/Event |
|------|----------------|
| 1990 | ◆ Pamela Tate assumes presidency of CAEL; CAEL headquarters relocate to Chicago, Illinois<br>◆ PLA remains at the core of CAEL's agenda while the organization expands outreach to, and services for, adult learners through workforce development programs |
| 1991 | ◆ National PLA survey conducted by CAEL resulting in the publication of *Prior Learning Assessment: Results of a Nationwide Institutional Survey* (Fugate and Chapman); 1,736 institutions responded<br>◆ Second edition of *Earn College Credit for What You Know* (Lamdin) published by CAEL |
| 1996 | ◆ National PLA survey conducted by CAEL resulting in the publication of *Prior Learning Assessment: A Guidebook to American Institutional Practices* (Zucker, Johnson, and Flint); 1,181 institutions responded and indicated some PLA practices were in place at their institutions<br>◆ Third edition of *Earn College Credit for What You Know* (Lamdin) published by CAEL |
| 2000 | ◆ CAEL launched on-line PLA verification program in collaboration with DePaul University |
| 2001 | ◆ The American Association of Collegiate Registrars and Admissions Officers, American Council on Education, and the Council for Higher Education Accreditation reissued endorsement of PLA and CAEL standards |
| 2006 | ◆ Fourth edition of *Earn College Credit for What You Know* (Colvin) published by CAEL<br>◆ Second edition of Assessing *Learning: Standards, Principles and Procedures* (Fiddler, Marienau, and Whitaker) published by CAEL<br>◆ National survey of PLA policies and practices conducted by CAEL |

**\*The following ten task force institutions together with ETS formed the first CAEL project. (Those shown in italics have portfolio samples in this book.)**

◆ Antioch College (now University)

◆ *Community College of Vermont*

◆ El Paso Community College

◆ *Empire State College*

◆ Florida International University

◆ Framingham State College

◆ Minnesota Metropolitan State College

◆ *New College, University of Alabama*

◆ San Francisco State College

◆ Thomas A. Edison College

# PRIOR LEARNING ASSESSMENT TODAY
## States of the Art

Judith B. Wertheim
Council for Adult and Experiential Learning

## INTRODUCTION

Over the past thirty years, individual postsecondary institutions throughout the United States have used Prior Learning Assessment (PLA) to recognize students' college-level learning outside the classroom and to award credit appropriately. Recently, endorsements for PLA have come from other quarters as well. At the same time that individual institutions are implementing PLA policies and practices, a growing number of state higher education systems, boards of regents, and other governmental departments are also encouraging PLA, particularly for adult learners.

The reasons for this additional support for PLA are clear. Those who hold postsecondary credentials are more likely to participate in the workforce than those with less than a high school diploma. Their earnings over a lifetime are significantly greater—a substantial personal benefit as well as a benefit to the state because of more taxable resources, fewer health problems, lower rates of crime, and greater civic engagement (Council for Adult and Experiential Learning, 2008, *Adult Learning in Focus: National and State-by-State Data*, pp. 12–20).

In addition, state policy makers are hearing the message that the United States—and individual states—*must* increase the numbers of post-secondary credentials if our country is to remain economically competitive in the world. As the Council for Adult and Experiential Learning (CAEL) points out in *Adult Learning in Focus: National and State-by-State Data*, "32 states cannot catch up to the educational attainment levels of the best performing countries internationally by relying solely on strategies related to traditional-age students—even if students in those states graduate from high school at the rate of the best performing state, even if high school students enter college at the rate of the best performing state, even if these students graduate from college at the level of the best performing state, and even if educated immigrants continue to enter the U.S. at the levels of the recent past. Educating adults must be part of the solution" (p. 7).

It is, however, not easy for many adults to return to school. Barriers to continuing education, which can be daunting, include accessibility, affordability, and aspirations (CAEL, 2008, *State Policies to Bring Adult Learning into Focus*). Consequently, the opportunity to earn credit for prior learning is especially appealing to adult learners and educators, because it helps overcome all of these barriers.

### ACCESSIBILITY

By offering the possibility of credit for prior learning acquired via corporate training, work experience, civic activity, and independent study, colleges and universities reach out to adult learners and find creative ways to help those learners return to school. This outreach effort makes the process easier and less forbidding.

### AFFORDABILITY

Earning credit for prior learning helps adult students earn their postsecondary credentials more quickly than they would otherwise, thus saving time and money. Moreover, costs are reduced when students avoid repetition of course material, frequently required if their comparable experiential learning is not recognized.

### ASPIRATION

By recognizing and awarding college credit for college-level learning, PLA acknowledges the academic value of experiential learning. Adults who have been away from the academic setting for some time thus understand that they can succeed at a postsecondary institution; they have already demonstrated that they are capable of college-level work.

## MEETING THE CHALLENGE

Although the pipeline of traditional students who follow the K–16 pathway is still the primary focus of federal and state educational policy makers, there are increasingly vigorous efforts throughout the country to encourage adults, especially those who have some college but no degree, to return to school. In this chapter, the efforts of four states (alphabetically, Kentucky, Minnesota, Oklahoma, and Pennsylvania) will be highlighted. These examples demonstrate how states can support PLA efforts in ways that are consistent with their unique academic culture, while simultaneously reaching for the common goal of increasing the educational attainment of their adult residents.

## Kentucky

Launched by the Council on Postsecondary Education (CPE) in 2007, the *Double the Numbers Plan* outlines statewide strategies for Kentucky to double the number of bachelor's degree holders in the state by 2020. As the plan explains, increasing bachelor's degrees is the quickest, most direct way for Kentucky to increase its economic prosperity (see http://cpe.ky.gov/doublethenumbers/). Among the specific target groups are working-age adults without a bachelor's degree. This group includes:

1. Adults who started but never completed a bachelor's degree
2. Adults with an associate's degree who want to complete a bachelor's degree
3. High school graduates with no postsecondary experience
4. GED completers with no postsecondary experience

The Kentucky Adult Learner Initiative is an effort to make the state's postsecondary sector more friendly to the adult learner. It is a partnership among state government, postsecondary institutions, and the private sector to help adult learners earn their degrees. The CPE surveyed members of the Kentucky Adult Learner Initiative Advisory Board, as well as participants at an adult learning summit in 2008, to identify the three priority areas for the project: credit for prior learning, financial aid, and flexible academic programming (M. Bell, personal communication, August, 11, 2008).

Clearly, in Kentucky, postsecondary institutions and other partners view PLA as a major incentive for adult learners. By involving its partners from the very beginning in planning PLA policies and practices, the Kentucky CPE hopes to "create a comprehensive policy framework at both the state and institutional levels to support adult learners" (http://cpe.ky.gov/policies/academicinit/adult_learner.htm).

## Minnesota

In 2007 the Minnesota State Legislature passed a Higher Education Fairness Statute, directing Minnesota State Colleges and Universities (MnSCU) to award credit for military training experience per the ACE guidelines or the equivalent. This legislation led to further discussion of PLA credit as part of a comprehensive plan by MnSCU, the Minnesota National Guard, and even the Minnesota Department of Employment and Economic Development to help adults complete their degrees with recognition of prior learning. The goal now is the articulation of a PLA policy—to be approved by the MnSCU Board of Trustees—that will apply to all institutions in the system (see http://www.mnscu.edu/board/materials/2008/may21/asa-05-proposed_335.pdf).

The process of developing this PLA policy for the Board has been a long one. In 2006 MnSCU surveyed the status of PLA throughout the system and a task force that included faculty, administrators, staff, and student representatives developed policies and procedures. By engaging a wide variety of participants, MnSCU was able to introduce the concept of PLA well in advance of implementation. Moreover, the draft policy and procedures have been reviewed by all institutions and other groups within the state educational leadership. This broad dissemination has provided many opportunities for input about PLA in Minnesota.

When the Board approves the policy, MnSCU plans statewide training to assist institutions with interpretation and implementation of both policy and procedures. The target date for implementing PLA system-wide is March of 2009 (L. Lade, personal communication, August 8, 2008).

## OKLAHOMA

*Reach Higher* is Oklahoma's degree completion program, a program that fully embraces PLA. Indeed, prospective students who are searching the website of the Oklahoma State Regents for Higher Education will find a very clear definition of PLA and of PLA practices:

> ### *Earn Credit Through Prior Learning Assessment*
>
> Recognizing that adult students bring a variety of experiences with them when enrolling in college, the Oklahoma Adult Degree Completion Program will work with students to assess any college-level learning they may have acquired.
>
> Through prior learning assessment (PLA), students will actively examine their own experiences in work, training and life experience that may qualify as college-level learning for college credit. The program will also evaluate students' educational goals to determine what learning they already have and what knowledge they need to gain in order to meet those goals.
>
> —Oklahoma State Regents for Higher Education
> http://www.okhighered.org/reachhigher/earn-credit.shtml

Indeed, Oklahoma has recognized the importance of "extra-institutional learning" for over thirty years. In 1972, the State Regents issued its first policy and has revised it several times since, most recently in 1995 (D. Blanke, personal communication, August 14, 2008). And the policy is still applicable.

According to the Oklahoma State Regents for Higher Education, " 'Extra-institutional Learning' is attained outside the sponsorship of legally authorized and accredited postsecondary institutions. The term applies to learning acquired from work and life experiences, independent reading and study, the mass media and participation in formal courses sponsored by associations, business, government, industry, the military and unions" (http://www.okhighered.org/student-center/college-stdnts/academic/extra-learning.shtml).

With a policy already in place, Oklahoma encourages PLA at all public postsecondary institutions in the state, and is encouraging faculty to advise students about the use of PLA, to implement PLA preparation classes, and to identify a group of content specialists on the campuses. The Regents are also exploring various options for expanding PLA implementation, such as a statewide assessment process.

## PENNSYLVANIA

The Pennsylvania State Board of Education formally endorsed PLA at its March, 2006 meeting. Moreover, PLA has been recommended jointly by Pennsylvania Departments of Education and Labor & Industry and promoted by Governor Edward G. Rendell as an integral part of *Job Ready Pennsylvania*, a workforce development initiative (http://www.paworkforce.state.pa.us/about/cwp/view.asp?a=471&q=152120).

In August, 2006, Governor Rendell endorsed PLA credit for continuing education students in all postsecondary institutions in Pennsylvania. Announcing his endorsement, the Governor said, "In today's global economy, more jobs than ever require some postsecondary education. Many Pennsylvanians have a wealth of hands-on experience and workforce skills, but they lack the educational credentials to advance. With this initiative, it will now be possible for people to get ahead based on the real-life skills and knowledge they've demonstrated and developed on the job" (http://www.paworkforce.state.pa.us/about/cwp/view.asp?a=470&q=156432).

In November, 2006, representatives of both private and public postsecondary institutions in the state participated in a summit that provided a forum to discuss the rationale, definition, and state policies for PLA. The goal of the summit was to establish a common ground in order to promote transferability and accessibility of PLA in Pennsylvania (http://www.paworkforce.state.pa.us/professionals/cwp/view.asp?a=11&q=157055).

In April, 2008, the Department of Education sponsored another statewide conference to share best PLA practices in Pennsylvania. Following this meeting, plans call for a state PLA policy that includes guidelines and standards for portfolio review. Although participation in PLA will be on a voluntary basis, postsecondary institutions will be encouraged to do so. To aid them in adopting PLA, the recommended policy and practices will be posted on the Department of Education website, which will also include a list of institutions that offer PLA opportunities, as well as those that accept transfer of PLA from other institutions (P. Unger, personal communication, August 4, 2008).

## CONCLUSION

Throughout the country, many states, in addition to the four cited here, are energetically moving forward to engage adult learners, to welcome them to postsecondary institutions, and to find creative ways to help them complete their education. These efforts acknowledge that, in order to be internationally competitive in the twenty-first century, our country must increase the number of credential and degree holders, and only by adding to the pool of successful adult learners can we meet this goal.

This brief review of four states indicates that there are many paths to the goal. Offering the opportunity to earn credit for prior learning is one of them; even here, however, variations abound. Some states, for example, have been offering PLA opportunities for many years; others are new at it. Some states have a PLA policy in place, but few implementation sites; others have continued to implement and refine PLA practices over the years. Some states seek uniform, statewide PLA policies and practices; others encourage individual institutions to develop their own policies and practices within general guidelines. Some states have involved faculty, staff, students, legislators, and others early in the PLA planning process; others still have internal and external marketing challenges before them.

Despite variations, however, the states that are part of the PLA community share some goals. All of these states are seeking innovative, academically sound practices to ensure that adults will succeed in the postsecondary world. With over thirty years of history, PLA is seen as a useful tool to help adults earn a degree, thereby enhancing their own personal satisfaction, as well as the state's economy and the country's future.

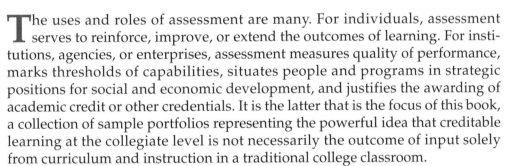

Morry Fiddler and Catherine Marienau
DePaul University

## ACCEPTANCE OF PRIOR-LEARNING ASSESSMENT

The uses and roles of assessment are many. For individuals, assessment serves to reinforce, improve, or extend the outcomes of learning. For institutions, agencies, or enterprises, assessment measures quality of performance, marks thresholds of capabilities, situates people and programs in strategic positions for social and economic development, and justifies the awarding of academic credit or other credentials. It is the latter that is the focus of this book, a collection of sample portfolios representing the powerful idea that creditable learning at the collegiate level is not necessarily the outcome of input solely from curriculum and instruction in a traditional college classroom.

The recognition of learning gained from experience is an outgrowth of the convergence of several factors, including: (1) a growing understanding of how individuals can and do learn from their experiences; (2) a respect for the demands on people's lives to both serve in multiple roles and be influenced by multiple contexts that lead to a rich storehouse of experience that may be mined for learning; and (3) the recognition by academic institutions that learning is bounded by neither time nor place. Since the 1970s, the emergence of "prior learning assessment" as a subset of assessment practices—represented worldwide by such acronyms as PLA, PLAR, APL, APEL, and others—has gained increasing attention to reduce redundancy and inefficiencies of requiring students to participate in one-size-fits-all curricula when they are otherwise qualified by knowledge or skills gained from experiences.

## TEN STANDARDS FOR ASSESSMENT, REVISED

The publication of *Assessing Learning: Standards, Principles, and Procedures* in 1989 by Urban Whitaker (CAEL) represented a critical effort to accomplish two significant goals simultaneously. One goal was the legitimization of assessment and its application to prior learning by grounding recommended assessment practices in a set of standards based on sound principles and a public declaration that formal instruction is not the only source of significant learning. The second goal was the validation of some assessment practices and the marginalization of others by setting forth a systemic basis for quality assurance at three different levels—standards, principles, and procedures, all aligned among themselves.

With great respect for the goals and the insight represented in the first edition, we approached the revision of *Assessing Learning* (2006) as an updating because of a growing understanding of learning, particularly learning from experience; a recognition that assessment was a term and activity gaining currency outside of academia (for whom the first edition was singularly directed); and our own observations and "lessons learned" from working with students and programs that had adopted or adapted some, if not all, of the standards. To these influences, we brought the point-of-view that the greatest potential for meaningful learning in any context lies in the examination of what we hold as beliefs, knowledge, habits, perceptions, and emotional responses as the basis for continuous learning from experiences, the essential premise of PLA.

The *ten standards* from the first edition of *Assessing Learning*, then, have been revised to embed these considerations:

◆ Promoting a major objective of education, particularly given the demands of a rapidly changing world: the development of learning how to learn well from experience;

◆ Broadening the application of assessment from academic credentialing to other contexts; and,

◆ Embracing the need for ongoing attention to both our competence (skills, knowledge and their application) as assessors and the presuppositions we bring to assessment.

What follows are the *ten standards for quality assurance* in *Assessing Learning* (2006). They are divided into two groupings, each containing five standards that address the assessment of learning per se and the quality assurance of administrative processes associated with an organized assessment program. Along with each standard, we have offered one or more questions to illustrate some of the significant inquiries and/or decisions that must be made to align practices and procedures with the standard.

## ACADEMIC STANDARDS

I. **Credit or its equivalent should be awarded only for learning and not for experience.**

◆ How do we know learning when we see it?

◆ How do we remain mindful of the distinctions between inputs and outcomes of learning and consistent in our discrimination of learning from experience per se?

II. **Assessment should be based on standards and criteria for the level of acceptable learning that are both agreed upon and made public.**

  ♦ How are we defining college-level learning?

  ♦ If we think first about "higher level learning," does that open up ways to think about this standard and criteria applicable to learning from experience that may complement common definitions in education or even be distinct from them?

  ♦ Are we public with our criteria and definitions with students? among ourselves?

III. **Assessment should be treated as an integral part of learning, not apart from it, and should be based on an understanding of learning processes.**

  ♦ Do we provide feedback that is likely to be understood and encouraging of further learning?

  ♦ Do we offer opportunity for learners to incorporate feedback into their demonstration(s) of learning?

  ♦ Do we revisit my/our understanding of the research about effective uses of assessment?

  ♦ How do we honor the premise that assessment is a part of learning while fulfilling the responsibilities of evaluating whether learning meets threshold levels of quality?

IV. **The determination of credit awards and competence levels must be made by appropriate subject matter and academic or credentialing experts.**

  ♦ Who is doing the assessing? What are the indicators of expertise?

  ♦ Who in the organization monitors the work of the credentialing experts?

V. **Credit or other credentialing should be appropriate to the context in which it is awarded and accepted.**

  ♦ Do we recognize learning that is not prescribed by a set curriculum that nevertheless fits a student's goals and is consistent with the intent of the curriculum?

  ♦ Do we extend the boundaries of assessable learning to the point that the meaning or intentions of the curriculum are compromised?

## ADMINISTRATIVE STANDARDS

VI. **If awards are for credit, transcript entries should clearly describe what learning is being recognized and be monitored to avoid giving credit twice for the same learning.**

  ♦ Should credit awards be annotated differently than instruction-based transcripting? Why?

VII. **Policies, procedures, and criteria applied to assessment, including provision for appeal, should be fully disclosed and prominently available to all parties involved in the assessment processes.**

  ♦ Are we clear enough in our policies, processes, and procedures, and the bases for them, to make them transparent?

VIII. **Fees charged for assessment should be based on the services performed in the process and not determined by the amount of credit awarded.**

- ◆ What is the financial model on which we operate our program(s)?
- ◆ Are we communicating promises regarding the awarding of credit for assessed learning, even implicitly?

IX. **All personnel involved in the assessment of learning should pursue and receive adequate training and continuing professional development for the functions they perform.**

- ◆ (How) do we contribute to a culture of learning around assessment?
- ◆ (How) do we promote a culture of mutual accountability around assessment?
- ◆ Do we manage our own learning about assessment or do we depend on our employer to provide direction?
- ◆ Does our organization provide substantive opportunities and support for ongoing professional development?

X. **Assessment programs should be regularly monitored, reviewed, evaluated, and revised as needed to reflect changes in the needs being served, the purposes being met, and in the state of the assessment arts.**

- ◆ Does our practice of assessment remain current?
- ◆ What assessment practices are we applying to ourselves?
- ◆ How would we demonstrate the quality of our assessment program?

## REALIZING THE STANDARDS

The value of these standards is only measurable by the extent to which each of them guides the decisions, policies, and procedures of assessors and administrators on the everyday level. A conscious decision to adopt the standards—or reject them but replace them with a different set—is the most practical starting point for bringing the standards to life. Not surprisingly, this conscious decision, and the discussions or debates that come with it, provide a foundation for aligning good policies with good practices.

# IDENTIFYING ASSESSMENT APPROACHES TO MATCH THE NEEDS OF THE STUDENT

Carolyn Mann
**Sinclair Community College**

## BEGINNING THE PRIOR LEARNING PROCESS

The assessment of prior learning allows a student who has gained significant learning through experiences from work, volunteer services, conferences, workshop attendance, in-service training, vocational interests, travel, independent reading, and the like, to have that learning evaluated for potential college credit via the development of a portfolio and other assessment methods. During my tenure as Director of Experience-Based Education and Coordinator for Lifelong Learning at Sinclair Community College in Dayton, Ohio, a system was developed to help students make better choices about prior learning assessment (PLA), particularly regarding which approaches to assessment to choose based on their experiential learning.

How does a student learn about PLA opportunities, and how do they "sign up"? Marketing, both formal and informal, is an integral part of the program. Students can learn about assessment through a variety of methods:

◆ Referrals from academic advisors and/or faculty

◆ Referrals from the admissions office

◆ Brochures and newspaper articles

◆ Advertisements in local newspapers that invite those interested to information sessions

◆ Direct mail pieces inviting interested parties to information sessions

◆ Referrals from former students

◆ Contact with employers, inviting employees to information sessions held at their worksite

◆ And, today, via the use of technology, especially the Internet

Prior learning assessment is not an appropriate option for everyone. Students must have a clear understanding of the process and how they may best fit into it. Pre-screening is essential, and students must be carefully advised about the amount of work involved, the need for good writing skills, and the risks of the process, i.e., there is no guarantee that credit will be awarded for prior learning simply for the presentation of a portfolio or taking an examination. Students learn, too, that their work will be submitted to faculty for final evaluation and determination of college credit awards. After this initial screening, students will better understand how, or if, they should proceed through the assessment options available to them.

The flow chart in Figure 1 entitled *PLA Advising and Administrative Guidance* has been updated from a previous edition, and provides a model integrating the various assessment options available to students.

## PORTFOLIO PROCESS

Students who decide to pursue an assessment of previous learning gained in non-traditional ways may select from a variety of options. Military personnel and veterans may find that they have gained college level learning through courses taken in the service. Others will find that proficiency examinations are the best option for them, especially for general education courses. There are many alternatives available.

There will be students, however, who decide that their best route to assessment is through the development of a portfolio.

They begin the process by participating in a specifically designed course, workshop, or seminar that will help them:

◆ Identify their learning from a variety of experiences

◆ Prepare portfolios equating their prior learning to college courses

◆ Develop educational plans

◆ Integrate prior and new learning to achieve their academic goals

As part of the portfolio development process, learners are introduced to various formats. Additionally, before submitting the portfolio for evaluation, the learner should minimally address these questions:

◆ Is the portfolio prepared in a professional manner, i.e., typing, spelling, writing style, neatness, etc.?

◆ Have all the required parts of the portfolio been included?

◆ Is the document correctly labeled?

The final step in the process is the evaluation of the student's portfolio by faculty with the appropriate subject-matter expertise. If needed, the faculty member may ask the student to demonstrate his or her competency in the subject matter or provide additional information.

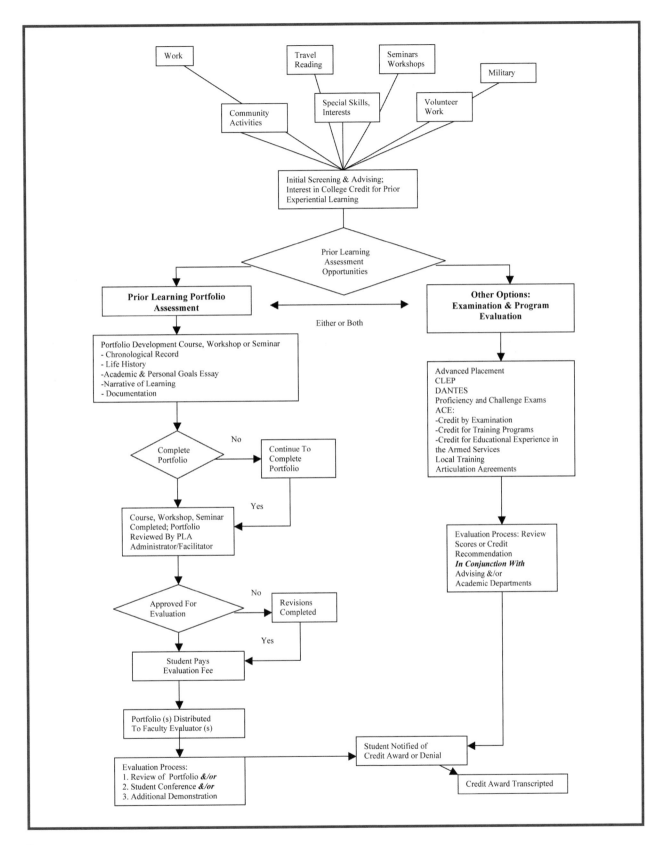

**FIGURE 1** ◆ PLA Advising and Administrative Guidance

From *Credit for Lifelong Learning* (5th ed.) by C. Mann, 1998, Bloomington, IN: Tichenor. Adapted with permission.

Preparing a portfolio is not an easy task. Students should carefully consider the educational value of the process and how the process directly relates to their achievement of academic goals (Willingham, 1977; Whitaker, 1989). The aim of the process should be to enhance the value of education for the individual.

Adults, time-conscious as they are, do not wish to replicate learning, nor be involved in an assessment process that they do not understand or cannot navigate. While prior-learning assessment allows both faculty and student to make maximum use of what the student has already learned and to build upon that learning, a clear understanding of how to participate in the PLA options is essential to everyone's satisfaction. The key to making the entire process work, then, is:

◆ Clear communication of the PLA program's availability

◆ Expectations of participants

◆ Directions for moving from beginning to end of whichever mode of assessment is selected by the student.

When understood by students, evaluators, other faculty, advisors, and administrators, a PLA Flow Chart, such as the one initially developed at Sinclair Community College, and presented in Figure 1, provides a clear and efficient route for students to follow in the assessment of their experiential learning.

**CHAPTER 5**

# ASHFORD UNIVERSITY®
### FOUNDED 1918 - CLINTON, IOWA

## Clinton, Iowa

"The mission of Ashford University® is to provide accessible, affordable, innovative, high-quality learning opportunities and degree programs that meet the diverse needs of individuals pursuing integrity in their lives, professions, and communities" (http://www.ashford.edu/info/). The University is regionally accredited by The Higher Learning Commission, of the North Central Association of Colleges and Schools (http://www.ashford.edu/info/accreditation.php).

## BRIEF HISTORY OF PORTFOLIO ASSESSMENT AT ASHFORD UNIVERSITY

A portfolio assessment program was implemented as a campus-based plan approximately 1998, when students were able to earn up to 32 credits through prior learning assessment (PLA). The criteria for the accelerated adult campus population is the same as the online Center for External Studies students (i.e., a maximum of 75 credits). The campus-based program is still in effect. In 2005, the University created the College of External Studies, and the PLA program was revised to reflect the needs of the growing non-traditional student population. The College of External Studies was renamed the Center for External Studies as of July 1, 2008.

In the Center for External Studies, up to 75 semester credits can be awarded for non-traditional learning in four ways: through national testing programs such as CLEP, DSST (DANTES), TECEP, Excelsior exams and Berlitz; through national credit recommendations such as ACE and PONSI; through sponsored professional training; and through the Experiential Essay process. Transcripts from national testing programs and national credit recommendations are processed through the Registrar while sponsored professional training and the experiential essay are processed through the PLA Department.

# ELIGIBILITY AND ACCESS

Potential Ashford University students can access the PLA Documentation Guide at *www.ashford.edu,* by clicking on "Online Programs," then "Transfer 99 credits" (Item 5, CD-ROM, Ashford University). New students with questions can access the same document from their Enrollment Advisor, and there is further information in the college catalog. Matriculated eligible students are referred by their academic advisor to enroll in the PLA Information Center on Blackboard. This center contains a variety of information including policies and procedures, CAEL standards, documentation requirements, explanation of fees, and directions for submitting credit requests.

Qualified PLA candidates must meet three criteria:

1. Successful completion of PSY 202 (a mandatory introductory Ashford University course)

2. Be fully matriculated

3. Have availability in the degree program for PLA credits

Ashford University also has specific quality assurance policies which apply to PLA:

◆ Students must be degree-seeking.

◆ PLA credit may not be counted toward the residency requirement in a degree program.

◆ PLA credit may be granted only in disciplines where Ashford University offers coursework or in disciplines related to its degree programs.

◆ PLA credit awarded at another regionally-accredited institution may be transferred to Ashford University with the approval of the Registrar and the PLA Director. These credits apply to the 75 credit maximum awarded for non-traditional learning in a degree program.

◆ Students in the Center for External Studies may apply up to nine non-collegiate credits toward their major as long as the content of the non-collegiate credit is comparable to the content of the course replaced.

◆ Students may use PLA credits to form the concentration in the BA Organizational Management degree if appropriate.

◆ Students may not use PLA credits to waive the Capstone Course.

◆ If the documentation is not written in English, a certified translation of all documents is required.

The *PLA Quality Assurance Model* (Item 6, on the CD, Ashford University) gives you a visual depiction of these policies and procedures.

# PRIOR LEARNING ASSESSMENT PRACTICES

There are two types of portfolio assessment: (1) Sponsored Professional Training (SPT) and (2) Experiential Essay. SPT is defined as formal structured coursework taken in a non-collegiate setting, as well as standardized training and national certificate programs, i.e., corporate training, in-service training, and continuing education. More definitively, a credit request for SPT requires that the student submit all of the following:

- ◆ Evidence of successful completion (official certificate or letter)

- ◆ Evidence of length of course (number of contact hours)

- ◆ Evidence of course content (syllabus, handouts)

- ◆ Contact information for the course instructor/work supervisor (current phone/email)

- ◆ Credit rationale paper (one page) for each submission/topic

Items 3 and 4, included on the CD-ROM, provide a sample credit rationale paper and documentation. Students interested in Sponsored Professional Training may review information on the PLA Information Center in Blackboard. There is also a discussion forum where students can post questions.

Conversely, [the] Experiential Essay is defined as a reflective paper (twelve to fifteen pages) that demonstrates understanding of the experiential learning process and the ability to organize one's reflections of a learning experience within the context of the Kolb learning style model. Through the essay process, students align personal experience with the learning outcomes of an accredited college course description. A sample portfolio and associated artifacts for a course, *Casino Operations* are included on the CD, Ashford University, Items 1 and 2.

Students must first take EXP 200, Fundamentals of Adult Learning (a three-credit elective course) in order to submit an Experiential Essay. (The course description is included on the accompanying CD-ROM, Ashford University, Item 7, *EXP 200 Experiential Essay Course Description*).

Experiential credit requests utilize a course equivalency model, where the eligible student selects a three-credit college level course from Ashford University or another accredited postsecondary institution. The student writes an essay that demonstrates knowledge equivalent to that which a student having taken the course would successfully display. Upon completion of EXP 200, the student may submit one or more essays for other PLA credit; each essay is also worth three credits. With the essay, students must provide documentation of at least one year of experiential learning related to the content of the request. This evidentiary artifact may be in the form of a publication, job performance report, business plan, work sample, photograph or validation of the experiential learning by an appropriate official. Only one artifact is required. The faculty assessor may approve or disapprove of the credit requested.

The application process is the same for both options. Students submit the appropriate documentation electronically through the PLA Credit Review Center, a site accessed through an Ashford University secure internet site. Once the student has officially registered and has submitted the documentation, the PLA submission is moved electronically through the Registrar, Finance, and Academic Departments. Refer to the flow charts presented in Figures 1 and 2, *PLA Submission Process* and *PLA Electronic Processing Center*, respectively.

All approved faculty assessors have expertise in the subject matter content and have been trained in the assessment process. The majority of assessors are full-time, campus-based faculty. As the need arises in a specific content area, part-time faculty and online faculty will be recruited.

Approved credits may be applied to elective, general education, or core requirements, depending on the content of the portfolio and the degree audit of the student. Sponsored Professional Training (SPT) credits are transcripted by topic while the experiential essay is recorded by the course title. No grade is awarded for either the SPT or Essay submissions. However, there is a grade for the EXP 200 course. The PLA Director monitors the questions in the PLA Information Center as well as teaches the EXP 200 course. In addition, any appeals/exceptions to the stated policies and procedures will be handled by the Director, Center for External Studies. There is no fee to enroll in the PLA Information Center (discussion board); however, students pay the regular tuition cost for the three-credit EXP 200 course. Currently, tuition is approximately $330 per credit hour.

The assessment fee for Sponsored Professional Training is $30 per credit hour requested and the assessment fee for the Experiential Essay is $125 per essay. There is no posting fee.

Faculty assessors are compensated at the rate of $10 per Sponsored Professional Training credit assessed and $30 per Experiential Essay assessed.

## USE OF TECHNOLOGY IN ASSESSMENT

There are four places where technology plays a role in the process of experiential learning assessment: the PLA Information Center, the EXP 200 course, the PLA Credit Review Center, and the PLA Electronic Processing Center.

1. The PLA Information Center uses the Blackboard platform. Once students are enrolled, they can read the various information, post questions in the discussion forum, and access the link to the PLA Credit Review Center.

2. The EXP 200 course is presented utilizing the Blackboard platform. The five-week course follows the structure and formatting of Ashford University's undergraduate online accelerated program. Students participate in weekly discussion forums, as well as upload weekly assignments.

The application process is the same for both Sponsored Professional Training and Experiential Essay. Students submit the appropriate documentation electronically through the PLA Credit Review Center, a site accessed through the Ashford University Intranet system. Once the student has officially registered and submitted the documentation, the PLA submission is moved electronically through the Registrar, Finance, and Academic departments.

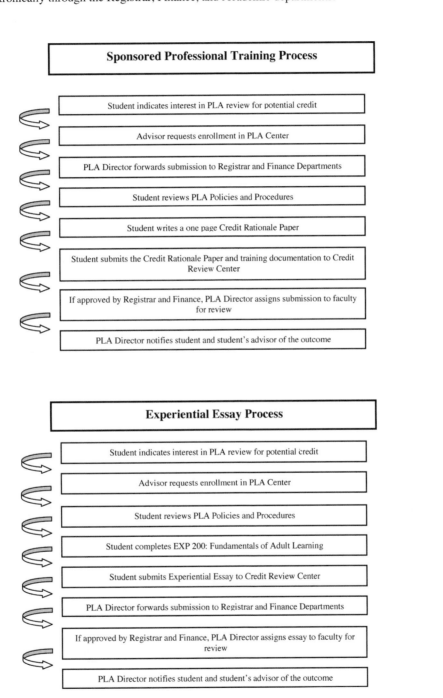

**Sponsored Professional Training Process**

Student indicates interest in PLA review for potential credit

Advisor requests enrollment in PLA Center

PLA Director forwards submission to Registrar and Finance Departments

Student reviews PLA Policies and Procedures

Student writes a one page Credit Rationale Paper

Student submits the Credit Rationale Paper and training documentation to Credit Review Center

If approved by Registrar and Finance, PLA Director assigns submission to faculty for review

PLA Director notifies student and student's advisor of the outcome

**Experiential Essay Process**

Student indicates interest in PLA review for potential credit

Advisor requests enrollment in PLA Center

Student reviews PLA Policies and Procedures

Student completes EXP 200: Fundamentals of Adult Learning

Student submits Experiential Essay to Credit Review Center

PLA Director forwards submission to Registrar and Finance Departments

If approved by Registrar and Finance, PLA Director assigns essay to faculty for review

PLA Director notifies student and student's advisor of the outcome

**FIGURE 1** ◆ PLA Submission Process
From Ashford University, 2008, Clinton, IA: Author. Adapted with permission.

# ASHFORD UNIVERSITY

| Status | Responsibility | Description |
|---|---|---|
| Not submitted | Student | Student has registered electronically but has not submitted required documents. |
| Submitted | PLA Director | Student submits PLA credit request. PLA Director uploads student's faxed documents that correspond with the submission. |
| Sent to Registrar | PLA Director | Registrar reviews student's credit request to verify that request does not duplicate previous/current coursework and will fit into degree pathway. |
| Registrar Reviewed <br>• Approved <br>• Denied | Registrar notifies PLA Director | Registrar approves or denies request based upon transcript review. If denied, rationale is noted. |
| Sent to Business Office | PLA Director | Business Office charges PLA fees to student's credit card. |
| Business Office Reviewed <br>• Processed <br>• On Hold | Business Office notifies PLA Director | Business Office processes billing or puts on hold if credit card is declined. |
| Sent to Faculty Assessor | PLA Director | PLA Director assigns submission to faculty assessor who reviews materials. |
| Evaluation Completed <br>• Approved <br>• Denied <br>• Approved pending rewrite | Faculty Assessor notifies PLA Director | Faculty reviews submitted materials and makes a credit recommendation: <br>• Awards or denies credit <br>• Number of credits awarded <br>• Upper or lower division <br>• Type of credit (elective, gen ed, or core) |
| *If needed*: <br>Approval pending rewrite (Experiential Essay only) | Student | Faculty assessor determines that <u>content is worthy of credit</u> but student needs to improve writing/mechanics. Student works with Writing Center, and student submits documentation to PLA Director from Center that rewrite is acceptable. |
| Sent to Registrar | PLA Director | PLA Director sends results to Registrar for posting on transcript. |
| Credits Awarded | Registrar | Credits are posted to the transcript. |
| Notification | PLA Director | PLA Director notifies student and academic advisor of results. |
| Process Completed | PLA Director | Submission is filed in electronic archives. |

**FIGURE 2** ◆ PLA Electronic Processing Center
From Ashford University, 2008, Clinton, IA: Author. Adapted with permission.

3. The PLA Credit Review Center is a password-protected secure website that requires students to register electronically. Students submit their request for credit, provide credit card information, and upload their PLA documentation through this website.

4. The PLA Electronic Processing Center is a password-protected section of the Intranet, an internal data management system. Only selected employees have access to this site. The PLA Director manages this site and assigns submissions to be reviewed by personnel in the Registrar, Finance, and Academic Departments.

## ASHFORD UNIVERSITY'S STATISTICAL PROFILE: 2006–2007

a. Total number of credits reviewed by portfolio assessment in the last academic year (Fall through Summer Sessions of the academic year) 2006–2007?
   ◆ Sponsored Professional Training: 355 credits
   ◆ Experiential Essay: 24 credits

b. Average number of credits awarded based upon all students receiving "portfolio-awarded" credits during the academic year 2006–2007?
   ◆ Sponsored Professional Training: 5 credits average; 339 total credits
   ◆ Experiential Essay: 3 credits average; 24 total credits

c. Total number of students at the institution during the academic year 2006–2007?
   ◆ Approximately 7,000
   ◆ NOTE: New students are enrolled weekly in the online programs.

d. Total number of students at the institution who participated in the Portfolio Assessment Program during the academic year 2006–2007?
   ◆ Sponsored Professional Training: 64 students
   ◆ Experiential Essay: 8 students

### CD-ROM, ASHFORD UNIVERSITY: ITEMS 1 TO 8

**CD-ROM**

1. Portfolio Sample: Experiential Essay, Casino Operations
2. Casino Operations Artifact
3. Healing Touch Credit Rationale Paper
4. Healing Touch Documentation
5. PLA Documentation Guide
6. PLA Quality Assurance Model
7. EXP 200 Experiential Essay Course Description
8. Assessment Outcomes

# Athabasca University

## Athabasca, Alberta, Canada

"Athabasca University, Canada's Open University is dedicated to the removal of barriers that restrict access to, and success in university-level studies and to increasing equality of educational opportunity for adult learners worldwide" (http://www.athabasca.ca/aboutAU/mission.php). As part of this goal, "Athabasca University (AU) makes it possible . . . to earn a university education regardless of where you live or work, or your commitments to careers or families. The University strives to remove the barriers of time, space, past educational experience, and, to a great degree, level of income."(http://www.athabascau.ca/aboutAU/)

## BRIEF HISTORY OF PORTFOLIO ASSESSMENT AT ATHABASCA UNIVERSITY

In 1986, the Experimental Project for the Assessment of Prior Learning, conducted by Dr. Geoff Peruniak, surveyed literature on prior learning assessment (PLA) and collected samples of practices considered to be appropriate background models for Athabasca University. A report issued in November, 1989 presented recommendations for the development of a prior learning process for Athabasca University. While PLA was a topic of discussion for various committees over a period of a few years, in September 1997 a draft policy was introduced. This draft called for the formation of the Centre for Learning Accreditation (CLA) that would have responsibility, oversight, and management of the PLA process. Simultaneously, in 1997, a steering committee was formed. Since that time, there has been continuous progress with ongoing revision of policy and procedures, the last as recent as 2008.

The Centre for Learning Accreditation currently manages the prior learning and portfolio assessment processes for all Athabasca University programs. The unit is composed of a Director and three staff members. Transfer and challenge-for-credit are currently handled in the Office of the Registrar.

## RECOGNITION OF EXPERIENTIAL LEARNING

At Athabasca University, portfolio assessment is referred to as Prior Learning Assessment and Recognition (PLAR). Key principles noted in the PLAR pamphlet are based on the beliefs:

"that learners

♦ must possess knowledge related to the program

♦ know and are able to apply theories and concepts used in that program

♦ have a capacity to analyze using data, theories and concepts

♦ can present knowledge clearly concisely and at a university level"

(http://priorlearning.athabascau.ca/documents/PLAR%20pamphlet.pdf).

There are two types of portfolio assessment at Athabasca University:

1. PROGRAM-BASED. If a student selects the program-based model, the student must demonstrate knowledge and skills in his/her field with a "macro" approach (see Item 1, *Portfolio Sample* on the CD-ROM, Athabasca University file). Prior learning is more broadly demonstrated as competencies in this model. Program-based portfolios constitute the majority of assessments at Athabasca University. Each program has its own set of program criteria although there are some similarities among sets of criteria (i.e., essential skills). Item 2 (also on the accompanying CD-ROM), *The Criteria Table Version for [a] Program* is one of the rubrics utilized. Appendix B: "Learning Summary Worksheet for Program-Based Learning Portfolios" (with a sample) is found in *A Prior Learning Assessment and Recognition (PLAR) at Athabasca University: A Handbook for Preparing Portfolios,* Item 6 on the CD-ROM is a template for students to use to demonstrate their competencies for their program. Appendix C of that *Handbook* has "Sample Program Assessment Sheets."

2. COURSE-BASED. Several university program areas prefer the course-based approach. Students using this method of portfolio assessment use course learning outcomes as their guide. The Centre for Learning Accreditation (CLA) maintains course learning outcomes. At Athabasca University, applicants seeking credit in business degrees and in areas of psychology are encouraged to submit course-based portfolios (http://priorlearning.athabascau.ca/by-portfolio.php).

Students are obliged by policy to create the type of portfolio that is preferred by their academic program. Item 3 (on the CD) is a sample worksheet for "Course-Based Portfolio Assessment." Further details can be found in the *Handbook.*

Most importantly, credit awarded by PLA must be university-level and related to the Athabasca University credential the students are seeking.

# PORTFOLIO ASSESSMENT PRACTICES

Ideally, Athabasca University students receive information about PLAR in the admission or orientation letters that they receive from the Registrar's Office. Students may also contact the advising or counseling units and/or information attendants to learn about PLAR at Athabasca University. The Centre for Learning Accreditation (CLA) likewise maintains a large and informative website at *http://priorlearning.athabasca.ca/index.php*, to which inquiring students are directed. CLA staff can also answer potential students' questions.

The Centre has multiple roles. The staff:

"1. Guides, directs, instructs and mentors PLAR participants through the process,

2. Locates assessor expertise for all undergraduate courses available for PLAR,

3. Maintains the assessor database,

4. . . . Trains mentors and guides content experts through the PLAR assessment process,

5. Receives and vets official letters of documentation arriving from PLAR participants' attestors,

6. Adds vetted and copied documentation materials to three copies of the portfolio,

7. Vets portfolios to determine completeness,

8. Determines appropriate assessors and distributes portfolios accordingly,

9. Requests necessary student records from Records Office to accompany portfolio materials,

10. Handles shipping, mailing, and return mailing procedures,

11. Receives, edits, compiles, clarifies assessors' comments,

12. Prepares final paperwork for PLAR participant and University, in consultation with Program advisors/chairs, Assessors, [and the] Registrar's Office personnel"

(Conrad, D., 2007, *Practicing PLAR . . .* , slide 2-4).

Another option that serves as an entrée for students who wish to develop an experiential learning portfolio on their own (with advisement) may be the portfolio preparation course, Psychology 205: Prior Learning Assessment and Portfolio Development, a three-credit, Junior-level class. The course is graded Pass/Fail, and the three credits are separate from those awarded as a result of assessing portfolios through the CLA. Faculty tutors, as part of their teaching load, instruct the portfolio preparation course. Students enrolled in Psychology 205 would be directed to the CLA website for information on the process for subsequent assessment of their portfolios, which are separate from the course.

All submitted portfolios are assessed, but not graded. The assessment is composed of both qualitative and quantitative evaluation based upon appropriately designed rubrics. Scores are calculated based on a pre-determined grid (see the CD-ROM, Items 2–5, and the Appendices in *A Handbook for Preparing Portfolios*). PLAR-awarded credit is transcripted as a block of credit with no course numbers or names given (e.g., "27 credits were award through PLAR").

Figure 1 entitled the PLAR Process demonstrates the many steps and potential participants involved in assessment development.

With the different approaches, it is important to keep all University informers current. Adult learners must be apprised of their options early on in their degree program so they may benefit from all assessment possibilities. An Athabasca University student who is enrolled in a program (i.e., who is not a "visiting" student simply taking courses) and who is deemed "active" (has taken courses within the preceding year) can submit a portfolio for PLAR assessment. These students must have completed all transfer credit arrangements prior to receipt of a PLAR assessment. Credits earned though PLAR do not count toward residency. Each program at Athabasca University has a maximum number of credits that may be assessed using the portfolio assessment option ranging from a low of six credits in the Bachelor of Arts program to thirty-nine credits in the Bachelor of Arts, Labor Studies Concentration. A range of twenty-one to thirty credits is normal for an Athabasca University four-year undergraduate (baccalaureate) degree.

Athabasca University uses assessment teams who work independently of each other. The program-based portfolio team comprises a minimum of three assessors. The course-based portfolio approach requires two assessors per course/content area. Assessors are generally drawn from university faculty, from other universities, and/or outside the university. Assessors are chosen for their subject-matter expertise and must be appropriately credentialed. Athabasca University employs approximately 150 assessors located locally and across Canada. At present, assessors are compensated at the rate of $42 per hour with one hour of payment per portfolio; note, however, that re-evaluation of this rate is on the agenda. Important documents for assessors to use in the process of their evaluation of portfolios include Items 2 through 5 on the CD-ROM, as well as other publications related to principles of assessment, policies, and procedures.

Students pay a $500 flat fee for the portfolio process. The fee covers all consultations with the CLA staff, mentoring through the process, the assessment, and all credit that is received as a result of the evaluation.

## USE OF TECHNOLOGY IN ASSESSMENT

Athabasca University is a distance learning institution, thus students can be all over the globe. All contact with students is delivered either by email and/or telephone. The portfolio document, although usually submitted in print, can be submitted on CD or via a website. Athabasca University does not yet have its own designated platform for e-portfolios but is working toward this goal.

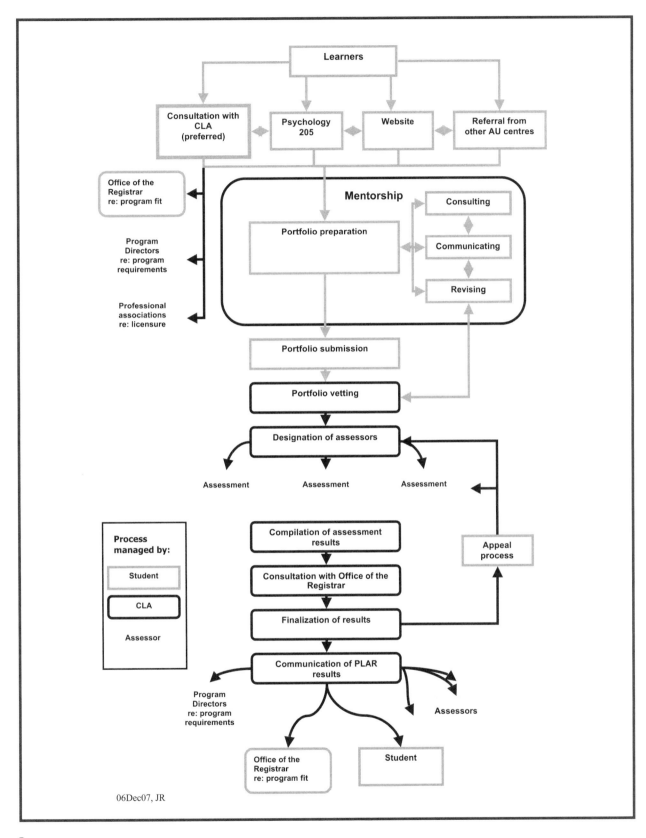

**FIGURE 1** ◆ PLAR Process

In the near future, Athabasca University intends to host software to accommodate e-portfolios, and develop a Moodle site to allow e-mentoring within a bounded community setting.

## ATHABASCA UNIVERSITY STATISTICAL PROFILE: 2006–2007

a. Total number of credits reviewed by portfolio assessment in the last academic year (Fall through Summer Sessions of the academic year), 2006–2007: There was the potential for a total of 2,793 credits to be awarded through PLAR. In other words, given the programs in which applicants were enrolled, the total available PLAR credit amount was 2793 (or 931 three-credit courses).

b. Average number of credits awarded based upon all students receiving "portfolio-awarded" credits during the academic year 2006–2007: The average is not a useful statistical figure for Athabasca University purposes. The total number of credits awarded through PLAR during this period however, was 2,304, or 82 percent of total credits possible.

c. Total number of students at the institution during the academic year 2006–2007: There were a total of 34,035 undergraduate students at Athabasca University during the referenced academic year. Of those, 13,656 were enrolled in a program and eligible to receive PLAR credit.

d. Total number of the students at the institution who participated in the Portfolio Assessment Program during the academic year 2006–2007: The total number of students who participated in the PLAR process was 108.

### ASSOCIATED WEBSITES

*http://priorlearning.athabascau.ca/index.php*

**CD-ROM**

### CD-ROM, ATHABASCA UNIVERSITY: ITEMS 1 TO 7

1. Portfolio Sample: Bachelor of Professional Arts-Human Services Program-Based Virtual Portfolio

2. Criteria Table Version for Program: Bachelor of Professional Arts-Human Services

3. Course-Based Assessment Form

4. Guidelines for Portfolio Assessors

5. Assessors' Response Sheet

6. Prior Learning Assessment and Recognition (PLAR) at Athabasca University: A Handbook for Preparing Portfolios

7. Assessment Outcomes

# CharterOak℠
## STATE COLLEGE
### Degrees Without Boundaries

From its inception in 1973, Charter Oak State College was established by legislative statute to "study, develop and coordinate" new methods of assessment for awarding college credit to associate and baccalaureate degree students. As a distance learning college, students may enroll at the institution and "create a personalized degree that takes into account their prior college experience, preferred method of earning credits, and future academic goals. The College is accredited by the Connecticut Board of Governors for Higher Education and the New England Association of Schools and Colleges" (http://www.charteroak.edu/AboutUs/).

## BRIEF HISTORY OF PORTFOLIO ASSESSMENT AT CHARTER OAK STATE COLLEGE

Initially, assessments of student experiential learning were conducted informally by college administrators and faculty; in 1992, a formal program of prior learning portfolio review was initiated. With this process, students were individually guided through the portfolio development process by the assessment coordinator. In the Fall term of 2006, the portfolio process changed. To gain credit for learning from experience, students are now required to enroll in an eight-week accelerated on-line portfolio development course.

Portfolio assessment is available to students matriculated at Charter Oak and other colleges, as well as to elementary and secondary school teachers who are seeking cross-certification in additional content areas, police and fire personnel seeking credit for promotion, and non-degree students seeking to document professional competencies.

Portfolio evaluation is part of a Prior Learning Assessment program that includes review of previous college transcripts; credit recommendations by ACE, PONSI, or Charter Oak State College reviews; standardized exams; special assessment of state and/or national certification or licensure awarded through testing.

## WHAT A PORTFOLIO IS AND IS NOT

Students can learn about Charter Oak State College's portfolio program in a number of ways. There is a "portfolio overview" on the institution's website, information about the program in the college catalog (also available online), and in the *Student Handbook*. (See also Item 6, *Student Information Sheet* on the CD-ROM.) "The portfolio process is an opportunity to document college-level learning acquired through life or work experience in areas for which there are no college-level exams. Credit is awarded for demonstrated knowledge and learning, not for experience" (http://www.charteroak.edu/Current/Forms/ StudentHandbook2007-2008.pdf, pp.13–14; and *Parts of the Portfolio*). A student in the process of applying for admission to the College, may contact an Admissions advisor; matriculated students can contact their Academic advisor and/or call or e-mail the assessment coordinator directly to request information about portfolio assessment. Non-matriculated students who have been referred by other colleges and universities, by the Connecticut Department of Education, or by community organizations are also encouraged to contact the assessment coordinator to obtain information about the portfolio program.

Portfolio assessment is based on evaluation of a document composed of five elements:

1. A description of a college course against which knowledge will be measured

2. A biographical introduction in which sources of learning in the individual's personal background are identified

3. A summary of the learning outcomes for the course being challenged

4. A narrative essay in which the student describes what he/she did and learned, and how that knowledge was applied

5. Evidence from a variety of sources to support the claim and to demonstrate knowledge and skills

"The portfolio is not a way to get credit for experience alone."
(http://www.charter oak.edu/Current/Programs/Portfolio/assessment.cfm)

## THE PORTFOLIO PROCESS

Steps in the process include:

1. Inquiry, where, for example, a student contacts the assessment coordinator and receives information about the portfolio process. (See Figure 1 entitled Portfolio Process Flow Chart.)

2. Enrollment in the portfolio course, IDS102: Prior Learning Portfolio Development. This is an eight-week, three-credit, accelerated, online course, during which a student is guided through the process of preparing a portfolio for one course for review. Upon successful completion of

**Portfolio Process Flow Chart**

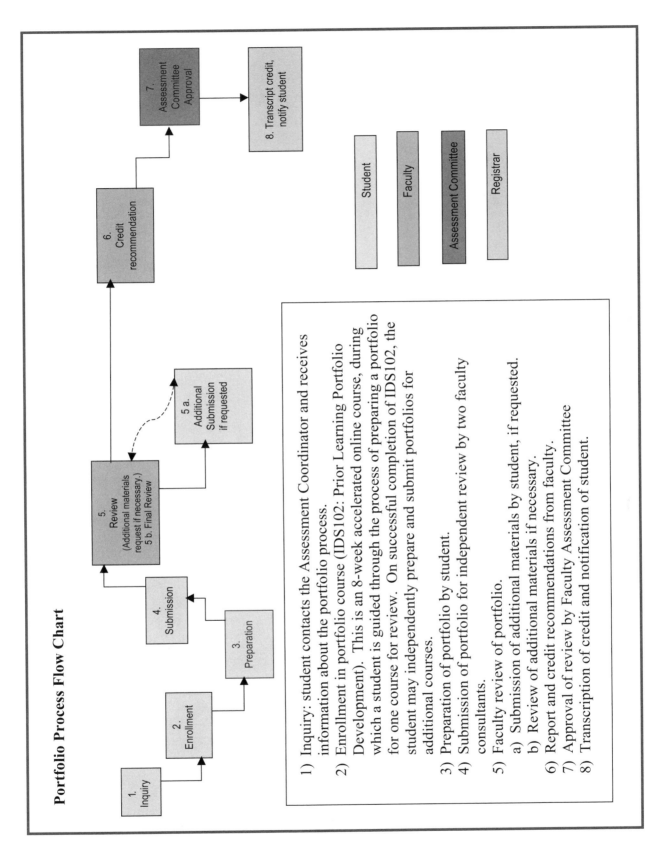

1) Inquiry: student contacts the Assessment Coordinator and receives information about the portfolio process.
2) Enrollment in portfolio course (IDS102: Prior Learning Portfolio Development). This is an 8-week accelerated online course, during which a student is guided through the process of preparing a portfolio for one course for review. On successful completion of IDS102, the student may independently prepare and submit portfolios for additional courses.
3) Preparation of portfolio by student.
4) Submission of portfolio for independent review by two faculty consultants.
5) Faculty review of portfolio.
   a) Submission of additional materials by student, if requested.
   b) Review of additional materials if necessary.
6) Report and credit recommendations from faculty.
7) Approval of review by Faculty Assessment Committee
8) Transcription of credit and notification of student.

**FIGURE 1** ◆ Portfolio Process Flow Chart

IDS102, the student may independently prepare and submit portfolios for additional courses.

3. Preparation of portfolio(s) by the student.

4. Submission of the portfolio to the Assessment Coordinator for independent review by two faculty consultants.

5. Faculty review of the portfolio.

   a. Submission of additional materials by student, if requested.
   b. Review of additional materials if necessary.

6. Report and credit recommendations from the faculty.

7. Approval of review by the Faculty Assessment Committee.

8. Transcription of credit and notification to student.

All students must first complete the six-credit English Composition requirement; they are then eligible to enroll in IDS102, the required portfolio course. The program is open to students at other institutions and non-degree seeking individuals as well. There is no age, GPA, matriculation or residency requirement for portfolio assessment, and Charter Oak State College accepts portfolio credit for all basic and upper level degree requirements, including general education and concentration areas. There is no limit on the number of portfolio credits that can be applied toward a degree at Charter Oak.

Some types of courses cannot be assessed. These include graduate courses and strictly experience-based courses such as practice teaching, internships, or practica. When standardized testing is available for a particular course, that is the preferred assessment recommendation and portfolio assessment is therefore not an option.

Although Charter Oak State College accepts portfolio credit in any amount and for any Charter Oak degree requirement, the credit earned must "fit" within the student's degree plan and not duplicate existing credit. If the student is planning to transfer the credits achieved via portfolio assessment, he/she must check with the receiving institution regarding any restrictions on the number of credits, levels, and uses of credit earned. It is the student's responsibility to ensure that the credit earned will be accepted toward the degree at Charter Oak or at the student's home institution.

## ASSESSMENT PRACTICES

To gain credit for learning from experience, students are required to enroll in IDS102: Prior Learning Portfolio Development. (See Item 2, *Syllabus* on the CD-ROM, Charter Oak State College.) During the three-credit course, students write a portfolio in one area of their choosing, and have the option of submitting the course packet for a credit review, without an additional fee. Upon successful completion of the portfolio course, students are free to develop more course portfolios on their own to submit for further review (*http://www.charter oak.edu/Current/Forms/StudentHandbook2007-2008.pdf*). Letter grades are awarded for the portfolio course itself, based on the student's written work and course discussion postings. Credit gained via portfolio review appears on a Charter Oak transcript as a grade of "P." Faculty members are instructed to recommend an award of credit only if the student achieves a grade level equivalent to "C" or better. The College warrants any "P" grade to be at the level of "C" or higher, making the "P" transferable to many institutions that would not normally accept pass/fail grades. Credit awards are posted to the student's transcript by the name of the course challenged, at the level and for the number of credits specified in the course description. "COSC does not grant block credit . . . (the) portfolio is a separate unit for each course requested. Each course requires a specific description, narrative and evidence, although in some cases evidence may serve to support knowledge claims for more than one course" (http://www.charteroak.edu/Current/Programs/Portfolio/faq.cfm#q1). No letter grade is given, and the portfolio credit does not factor into a student's grade point average.

Each portfolio is independently reviewed by two content area faculty experts who are currently teaching at a regionally accredited institution of higher education. Faculty reviewers may be teaching full or part-time at a two- or four-year institution. They are drawn primarily from colleges and universities in Connecticut, but may occasionally be drawn from institutions in other states when special expertise is needed. Faculty reviewers provide a written report for each course evaluated. Students receive a copy after the assessment is completed. Once the credit award has been approved by the Faculty Assessment Committee, the Registrar records the credits on an official transcript.

Tuition for the portfolio course is set at the current per-credit rate for resident or non-resident tuition, plus the current registration fee. During the fiscal year 2008 rates were $40 registration fee (per semester, for any number of courses); $531 for Connecticut resident tuition and $751 non-resident tuition. Tuition covers the cost of the online course, course materials, and review of the first course portfolio. Additional portfolios may be submitted for review at any time after the course has been successfully completed. The fee for additional portfolio reviews is $85 per credit attempted for matriculated students and $100 per credit attempted for non-matriculated students. There are no other fees associated with portfolio assessment or transcripting of credit awards.

Faculty evaluators are compensated according to the number of credits in the courses reviewed. Faculty evaluators submit a current curriculum vita for our files, and receive a letter of appointment as a Special Consultant for a term of approximately three years. During that period, there is no obligation to perform additional reviews if called upon, but the faculty member may do so if he/she chooses. A small honorarium is offered; the amount depends on the total numbers of credits in the course reviewed. The payment schedule effective until July 1, 2008 was as follows:

| Credits | Payment |
| --- | --- |
| 1–6 | $110 |
| 7–12 | $180 |
| 13–18 | $230 |
| 19–27 | $290 |
| 28+ | $340 |

For further details regarding faculty policies and procedures, see Item 4, *Faculty Guidelines for Portfolio Assessment,* on the accompanying CD-ROM (M. LeGrow, personal communication, July 15, 2008).

## USE OF TECHNOLOGY IN ASSESSMENT

The Prior Learning Portfolio Development course is taught online, incorporating some internet-based content. The course is entirely web-based. Electronic submission of a first draft of the portfolio is a course requirement, but students have the option of submitting the finished portfolio as a CD-ROM, electronically, or in paper format. This is to accommodate students who do not have the capability of scanning documentation, sending or receiving large documents, or creating CD-ROMs; who do not have access to equipment for converting video to DVD format; or who need to submit audio, video, or other visual documentation that would not reproduce well in transmittable electronic format.

Students also use e-mail as their primary means of communication with the IDS 102 course instructor and the Assessment Coordinator.

## CHARTER OAK STATE COLLEGE STATISTICAL PROFILE: 2006–2007

**a.** Total number of credits reviewed by portfolio assessment in the last academic year (Fall through Summer sessions of the academic year) 2006–2007: 384 credits

**b.** Average number of credits awarded based upon all students receiving "portfolio-awarded" credits during the academic year 2006–2007: 11 semester hours

**c.** Total number of students at the institution during the academic year 2006–2007: 1,672 students

**d.** Total number of the students at the institution who participated in the Portfolio Assessment Program during the academic year 2006–2007: 114

**CD-ROM**

### *CD-ROM, Charter Oak State College: Items 1 to 7*

**1.** Portfolio Sample: Pedagogical Grammar

**2.** Syllabus: IDS 102 Prior Learning Portfolio Development

**3.** Student Handbook
(*http://www.charteroak.edu/Current/Forms/StudentHandbook2007-2008.pdf*)

**4.** Faculty Guidelines for Portfolio Assessment

**5.** Parts of the Portfolio

**6.** Student Information Sheet

**7.** Assessment Outcomes

# EMPIRE STATE COLLEGE

## STATE UNIVERSITY OF NEW YORK

## Saratoga Springs, New York

Founded in 1971, Empire State College, State University of New York, is one of the university's 13 colleges of arts and sciences, accredited by the Middle States Commission on Higher Education and uniquely designed to serve adults pursuing associate, bachelor's and master's degrees onsite at 35 locations in New York state and abroad, as well as entirely online (http://www.esc.edu/esconline/online2.nsf/html/isescforyou.html).

## BRIEF HISTORY OF PORTFOLIO ASSESSMENT AT EMPIRE STATE COLLEGE

The evaluation of experiential learning has been an integral part of Empire State College from its opening in 1971. Empire State College is committed to the idea that people should be awarded credit for verifiable college-level learning regardless of where or how it was acquired. Many Empire State College students have gained knowledge from sources that are not validated in traditional classrooms, standardized examinations, or noncollegiate sponsored learning. Knowledge from sources such as workplace training, seminars, volunteer activities, or independent study is just as valuable as knowledge gained through more formal or standardized learning experiences. Such knowledge is often referred to as experiential learning.

Credit may be granted for verifiable college-level learning—knowledge or skills—acquired through life or work experience but not for the experience itself. Empire State College does not award credit simply for what has been done, even if it has been done for a long time and done well. For example, a student who has worked as an office manager for ten years will not be awarded credit simply for having ten years of office management experience. However, the student might earn credit for demonstrated learning about office administration, supervision, and office technology (*Student Degree Planning Guide*, 2007, p. 31).

The evaluation of such non-collegiate-based learning can take place in different ways (for example, by standardized examination), but at the heart of Empire State College's prior learning assessment (PLA) program is the use of the *individualized* prior learning assessment. This serves as the basis upon which expert evaluation of that learning is carried out.

## RECOGNITION OF EXPERIENTIAL LEARNING

Every student at Empire State College works with a primary mentor to design an individualized degree program proposal—the student's curriculum for the degree. Students also complete an educational planning study, which takes them through the degree planning process in detail. Within the degree program proposal design process, students determine advanced standing credits (up to ninety-six credits) that they will transfer in; some or all of these credits can be obtained by individualized PLA. Transcripted credit from previously attended accredited institutions, as well as credit-by-evaluation, such as pre-evaluated sources (e.g., standardized examination, certifications, licenses, etc.) can also be part of a student's "advanced standing."

For a student to request individualized PLA, the student first works with the assigned mentor to identify the college-level prior learning that the student may have. The student then develops a request, which usually includes an essay and supporting materials for each component of his or her prior learning (multiple submissions are permissible) that is submitted as a PLA request. This request will also include the draft of the degree program proposal, including its rationale. The request is reviewed by the mentor and then submitted through the mentor to the Center Office of Academic Review (COAR), where it is also reviewed. Once COAR has approved the submissions, an appropriate subject-matter evaluator is assigned to assess the learning.

The evaluator and the student meet (in person, by phone, and/or by e-mail) and further discuss the student's learning in a specific area. This interview is a critical part of the review process because it allows the evaluator to get a more in-depth view of the student's learning beyond the submitted materials. An evaluator can request that the student submit additional materials or revise the essay based on the interview.

As stated in Empire State College policy documents (available online):

"In formulating a prior learning recommendation, the evaluator

◆ Reviews the student's request and any supporting materials

◆ Interviews and/or consults with the student, and

◆ May ask the student to provide additional supporting materials or documentation of his/her learning. Demonstrations of learning may take a variety of forms, such as portfolios of creative work, annotated bibliographies of relevant readings, analytical essays, analysis of case studies, video/audio tapes of presentations, grant proposals, work products or training materials created by the student, etc."

(http://www.esc.edu/ESConline/ESCdocuments/policies.nsf/allby subject/Individual+Prior+Learning+Assessment+Policy+and+Procedures, . . . Evaluation Process and Credit Recommendation . . .)

The evaluator then writes a "Prior Learning Evaluation" recommendation. (see Item 2 on the CD-ROM, entitled *ESC*.)

"Written prior learning recommendations should meet the following criteria:

◆ Describe the methods used to evaluate the student's learning,

◆ Describe the specific elements of the student's learning,

◆ Indicate whether the learning is introductory or advanced level and provide a justification for advance level credit, when necessary,

◆ If the learning falls within the liberal arts and sciences, provide a justification for liberal arts and sciences credit, when necessary,

◆ If the learning meets one or more of the SUNY general education requirements, in part or in full, and provide a justification, when necessary,

◆ Assess any possible redundancy or duplication with other components in the student's degree plan, when necessary,

◆ Provide an appropriate title that describes the student's learning (not an experience, training, job or programs the student completed), and

◆ Recommend a semester-hour credit award for the student's learning

◆ An evaluator may recommend the amount and kind of credit requested, or may recommend more, less or no credit . . . The director of academic review for the center ensures that the evaluator's recommendations meet the college's criteria . . . The center assessment office provides a copy of the evaluator's recommendation to the student and the mentor, making clear that the recommendation is not an award of credit . . . Faculty of the college through the center program review committee can approve the award of prior learning credit by the college. The college awards prior learning credit following the approval by the faculty, and a technical review of the degree program and portfolio by the Office of College-wide Academic Review . . . Once OCAR clears the portfolio, the center decision becomes official."

(http://www.esc.edu/ESConline/ESCdocuments/policies.nsf/Allbysubject /individual+Prior+Learning+Assessment+Policy+and+Procedures, . . . Evaluation Process and Credit Recommendation . . .).

As a note of clarification, at Empire State College the term "portfolio" describes the full packet of information and materials assembled for the degree program proposal; the PLA evaluator report is one component of the portfolio. The PLA submission is called a "PLA request" to distinguish it from the degree program proposal (i.e., portfolio), which contains the student's essay and supporting materials (including the degree program rationale) that is used by the evaluator, in conjunction with an interview, to assess the prior college-level learning.

Empire State College uses a variety of practices to inform the student about the PLA process. Initially, students learn about PLA through recruiters, ongoing "information sessions" held throughout the State of New York, new student orientations, and meetings with their assigned mentor. At some new student orientations, a mini workshop is offered to explain the PLA process within the context of the self-designed degree program proposal. The college brochures, website, and catalog also explain the process briefly; the college publications, *A Student Guide: Credit for Prior College-Level Learning* and *Student Degree Planning Guide* describe PLA in detail.

Once students have begun their studies at Empire State College, they can attend a PLA workshop given at their local center. In this optional workshop, students learn the details of the PLA process. All students enroll in a study called Educational Planning, which is the only required study for all undergraduates and guides the students through the process of creating a degree program proposal. Within this study, students learn in detail about the PLA process and begin to develop their PLA requests. Students design and finalize their PLA requests working one-on-one with their mentor.

## ASSESSMENT PRACTICES

All matriculated undergraduate students are eligible for PLA. Credits awarded through the PLA process are considered "advanced standing" within the degree program proposal. Students are allowed to apply up to ninety-six credits of advanced standing of the 128 credits required for a bachelor's degree and up to forty credits of advanced standing of the sixty-four credits required for an associate's degree. Advanced standing credits represent all learning on a degree program proposal acquired before attending Empire State College, and can be a combination of transcript credit and credit by evaluation [which also includes credit by examination and pre-evaluated credits, such as American Council on Education (ACE) and National Program on Non-collegiate Sponsored Instruction (NPONSI) recommendations]. The degree program proposal, and thus any PLA, must be submitted for review before the student begins the last sixteen credits in his or her proposed program.

The PLA requests are reviewed at five different levels. First, the student's mentor (a faculty member) works with the student to create appropriate PLA documents and materials and reviews the final PLA requests. Revisions are made with the student as necessary. The PLA request is submitted to the COAR and specialized staff reviews the PLA request prior to assigning an evaluator. If the Center Office of Academic Review (COAR) staff determines that revisions are necessary, they work with the student and his or her mentor prior to assigning an evaluator. The student submits a PLA request per component (topic) and, in most cases, each is evaluated separately.

Once approved by the COAR staff, the PLA request is assigned to an evaluator. Empire State College uses a variety of evaluators, matching the expertise and experience with the academic area to be assessed. Evaluators are drawn from an inside pool (trained faculty, both full- and part-time) and from outside the college (individuals in the community with requisite expertise who are then trained by the college). Many times the outside evaluators are faculty at other colleges and universities. Some evaluators are shared across the state, especially in less common academic areas.

When the evaluator submits the report, the Center Office of Academic Review staff first reviews it before it goes back to the student and mentor. When the PLA request becomes part of the degree program proposal, the evaluator reports are reviewed by a faculty committee within the context of the overall degree portfolio. In addition, the Office of College-wide Academic Review (a college-wide centralized office) also reviews the evaluator reports as part of the final review process and for acceptance of student degree program proposals (see Figure 1 entitled PLA Process Flow Chart).

There are both non-credit workshops and a for-credit study within which the PLA process is taught. At each center, the COAR staff conducts PLA workshops. These are free and optional to the students and are focused on the overall PLA process. All undergraduate students also take a required educational planning study that takes the student through the individualized degree program planning process. Within the study, the process by which PLA requests are developed are discussed in detail and, as an outcome of the study, the student develops his/her requests as appropriate to the student's prior college-level learning. The student takes at least four credits and up to eight credits of educational planning, which can take many forms depending on the program in which the student is enrolled and the judgment of a mentor about a particular student's academic needs. The educational planning study is evaluated (by narrative and sometimes by narrative and letter grade both), but the degree program proposal and PLA requests are not.

In the workshops and in these studies, students are given two free publications that describe the PLA process in detail: *A Student Guide: Credit for Prior College-Level Learning* and the *Student Degree Planning Guide, 2007–2008* (see Items 4 and 5 on the CD-ROM, entitled *ESC*).

The COAR staff, as part of their responsibilities, teach the PLA workshops. Faculty, as part of their workload, teach the educational planning studies. The educational planning study is evaluated by the mentor responsible for that study, but the PLA requests are not nor are the PLA workshops graded.

All credit awarded for PLA requests are treated as advanced standing credit. Each request is one component and is transcripted as a credit-bearing individualized study with a specific title that has been agreed upon, under the category "credit by evaluation." (see Item 4 on the CD-ROM, *A Student Guide: Credit for Prior College-Level Learning,* p. 14; and Item 5, *Student Degree Planning Guide, 2007–2008,* p. 31).

All matriculated students are charged a "portfolio assessment fee" (currently $300), which covers the administrative costs of the individualized degree program. In addition, the "individual evaluation fee"(also currently $300), is charged to undergraduate students who request individualized credit by evaluation services, regardless of the number of PLA requests submitted. The fee is charged at the beginning of the second matriculated enrollment and supports the individual evaluation of prior learning service. The fee is automatically charged unless the student chooses not to receive any individualized credit by evaluation services.

The orientations and workshops are provided to students free of charge. The educational planning study (for most students, this is a four-credit study) is charged at the normal tuition rate, currently $181 per credit for New York State residents up to eleven credits (non-resident tuition is currently $442 per credit). There is a set rate for students taking twelve or more credits. There are no additional fees associated with the completion and approval of the PLA credits, that is, posting fees.

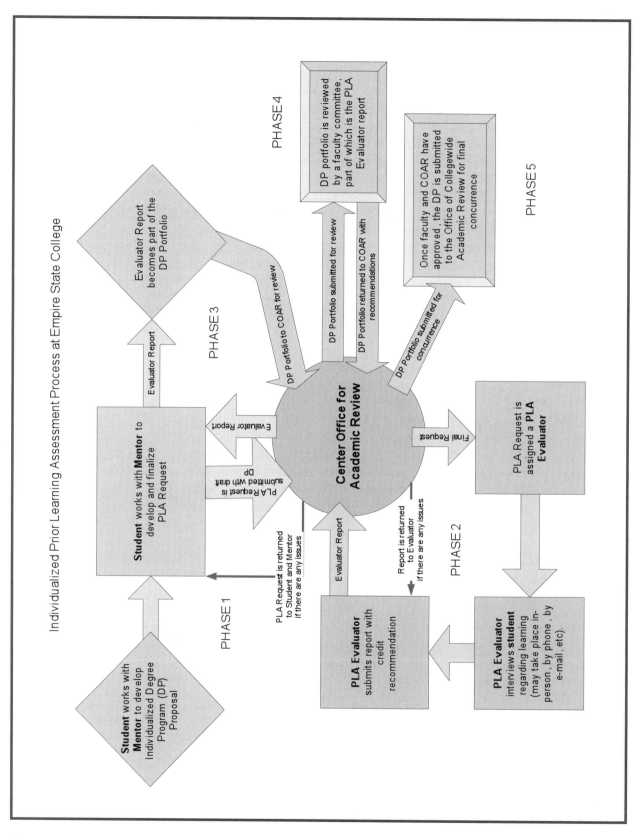

Individualized Prior Learning Assessment Process at Empire State College

**FIGURE 1** ◆ PLA Process Flow Chart

Evaluators are paid based upon the size and complexity of the credit request using the college's current compensation model. There is a maximum of twenty credits that an evaluator can assess for a given student without additional approval by COAR. The limit helps to "support the institutional integrity of the prior learning assessment process by ensuring that no single person evaluates too much of a student's overall degree program" (http://www.esc.edu/ESConline/ESCdocuments/policies.nsf/allbysubject/Individual+Prior+Learning+Assessment+Policy+and+Procedures, Individual Prior Learning Assessment Policy and Procedures, . . . Limits on Prior Learning . . .).

## USE OF TECHNOLOGY IN ASSESSMENT

The mode of delivery of mentoring, educational planning, degree program planning, and PLA varies across the college. Many use e-mail and on-line methods for communicating and delivery. For example, students who attend the Empire State College Center for Distance Learning may be located anywhere in the world and will be engaging in the entire process on-line. In other Empire State College centers, many faculty use the on-line environment to supplement the process and communication with their student. E-mail, fax, and phone calls are staples for many mentors and students as modes of contact and communication. The educational planning study can be conducted individually or in small groups, face-to-face or on-line, or some in combination of these methods.

Technology is used throughout the degree planning proposal process. The majority of students and mentors use a web-based program created by Empire State College to assist in the designing of the degree program proposal by keeping an ongoing record of studies to be incorporated in degree program proposals, within which the component title for the PLA request is logged. All degree program proposals are logged and tracked throughout the process in a database once the degree program proposal is submitted by the mentor. The results of the PLA request are logged, as are the results of the degree program proposal.

At present, Empire State College is creating a program that will allow students, mentors, COAR, and evaluators to manage the PLA process even better. This program will be web-based and will allow the student to design and submit electronically the PLA request and all supporting materials with the program. The request will follow the same procedures for review and evaluation with communication tools built into the program. The evaluator will also submit the evaluation report through the program. The "PLA Planner" is estimated to be in pilot phase by fall 2008 and full implementation by fall 2009.

There is another program currently under design at Empire State College that will electronically capture all available credit for a student. All incoming transcripts and documentation supporting prior learning will be entered into the program, along with critical information needed to evaluate the learning. The PLA requests will also be logged in this program as potential available credit. Students and mentors will have access to reports that list all potential available credit that the student can use for advanced standing in designing his or her degree program proposal.

a. Total number of credits reviewed by portfolio assessment in the last academic year (Fall through Summer sessions of the academic year) 2006–2007: 83,355*

b. Average number of credits awarded based upon all students receiving "portfolio-awarded" credits during the academic year 2006–2007: 38.0*

c. Total number of students at the institution during the academic year 2006–2007: 16,825 undergraduate; 17,621 total

d. Total number of the students at the institution who participated in the Portfolio Assessment Program during the academic year 2006–2007: 2,193 received credit*

## ASSOCIATED WEBSITES

### Assessment Resources

*http://www.esc.edu/esconline/across_esc/assessment.nsf/home.html*

### CDL Credit for Prior Learning

*http://www.esc.edu/esconline/across_esc/cdl/cdl.nsf/wholeshortlinks2/Credit+for+Prior+Learning*

**CD-ROM**

## CD-ROM, EMPIRE STATE COLLEGE: ITEMS 1 TO 7

1. Portfolio Sample: Environmental Advocacy, Organizing and Research, Excerpt

2. Prior Learning Evaluation (Faculty Evaluation), edited Excerpt

3. Individual Prior Learning Assessment Policy and Procedures

4. A Student Guide: Credit for Prior College-Level Learning

5. Student Degree Planning Guide, 2007–2008

6. Fact Sheet, February 2008

7. Assessment Outcomes

---

\* These numbers represent credits earned by students participating in credit-by-evaluation, which includes individualized prior learning as well as prior learning evaluated through formalized examinations (e.g., CLEP, TECEP, etc.) and pre-evaluated learning through outside agencies such as ACE and NPONSI and Empire State College's pre-evaluated learning. Currently, Empire State College data systems are unable to separate these types of evaluation; better data reporting is currently being developed.

## CHAPTER 9

## Denver, Colorado

[Since 1877] "Regis University . . . has been meeting the needs of students through innovative classroom-based or online programs centered in academic excellence. Regis University's commitment to the individual student is fostered through the heritage of our values-centered Jesuit education. Today more than 16,000 students call Regis University home. This Colorado-based university is comprised of three Colleges: Regis College, the Rueckert-Hartman College for Health Professions, and the College for Professional Studies, and offers classes in a campus-based setting as well as online programs in a range of studies." (www.regis.edu). A Jesuit university, Regis "encourages all members of the Regis community to learn proficiently, think logically and critically, identify and choose personal standards of values, and be socially responsible." (http://www.regis.edu/regis.asp?sctn=abt).

## BRIEF HISTORY OF PRIOR LEARNING ASSESSMENT AT REGIS UNIVERSITY

Regis University began undergraduate and graduate programs for adult students in 1978. The Prior Learning Assessment (PLA) Program, begun in 1980, includes both a Testing Center and a Portfolio Program, both options highly promoted to over 5,300 undergraduate students. Students may combine transfer, testing, and portfolio credits in the undergraduate degree plan for a total of ninety-eight of the 128 semester hours required for the degree. In any event, the course entitled ED 202: Prior Learning Assessment is the key to beginning and understanding the PLA process. Aside from the course, one can learn about the Regis approach through its website information, especially the site on Policies and Procedures (*http://academic.regis.edu/ed202/policies.htm#Specific%20Regis%20Academic%20Degree%20Requirements*) used extensively in this report. An overview of the PLA portfolio process is illustrated in the flow chart given in Figure 1.

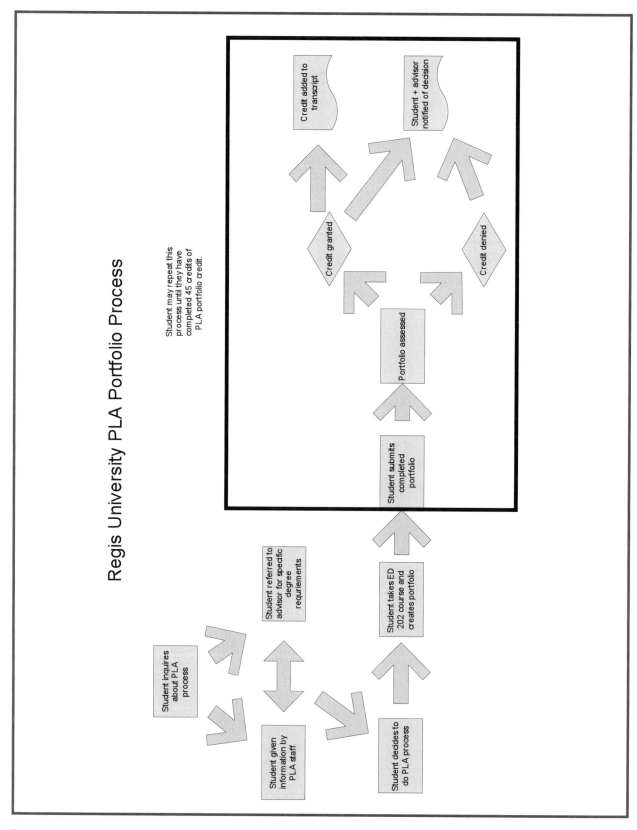

## Regis University PLA Portfolio Process

Student may repeat this process until they have completed 45 credits of PLA portfolio credit.

Credit added to transcript

Student + advisor notified of decision

Credit granted

Credit denied

Portfolio assessed

Student submits completed portfolio

Student referred to advisor for specific degree requirements

Student takes ED 202 course and creates portfolio

Student inquires about PLA process

Student given information by PLA staff

Student decides to do PLA process

**FIGURE 1** ◆ Regis University PLA Portfolio Process

## LEARNING ABOUT PLA AT REGIS

Current students learn about PLA and portfolio assessment primarily through their academic advisors. New and prospective students can learn about these opportunities on the Regis University website (*www.regis.edu*), as well as through the online New Student Orientation (*http://spsundergradorientation.org*).

## PLA PRACTICES AT REGIS

### ELIGIBILITY FOR PLA

Students eligible for portfolio assessment must be degree-seeking undergraduates. The only exception to this eligibility policy is for teacher education students doing licensure courses only. Students may complete forty-five of the 128 credits required for graduation through the portfolio process. Portfolio credits may satisfy any part of the degree (i.e., liberal arts core, major, minor, or electives) in accordance with residency requirements for their degree. There is no GPA or age restriction for portfolio students.

### PORTFOLIO ORIENTATION

Regis provides a three-credit course, ED 202 Prior Learning Assessment, which teaches the basics of designing, writing, and submitting the portfolio. During the course, students study theories of how adults learn, components of writing and documenting the portfolio, and submission of their portfolios electronically using iWebfolio software. The course is offered in both classroom and online format (*http://academic.regis.edu/ed202/jobaids/stuacctsetup.htm*).

The PLA course is taught by university faculty, some part-time and some who use this course as part of their contractual load.

### PORTFOLIO ASSESSORS

Students match their learning to a course description from any regionally accredited college or university. Portfolios are assessed by faculty approved to teach the identified course. The majority of faculty members are part-time affiliate (adjunct) faculty. If there is no Regis faculty member qualified to assess a particular portfolio, a faculty member at another accredited college or university will be contacted (*http://academic.regis.edu/ed202/policies.htm#STANDARDS %20FOR%20AWARDING%20CREDIT%20THROUGH%20PRIOR%20LEARN ING%20ASSESSMENT*).

### GRADING THE PORTFOLIO

The portfolio is assessed using an established rubric and scored on several elements using a 1-to-5 (1 = poor, 5 = superior) rating scale. The portfolio must receive an average score of 3 on all elements to "pass" and gain the petitioned credit. This score is separate from the grade for the ED 202 Prior Learning Assessment course.

In reviewing a portfolio, the assessor has the following options: grant credit as petitioned; grant credit for content with another course title (e.g., a student may have learning equivalent only to the Training and Development course rather than the Human Resource Management course, which is more comprehensive); require the student to submit an addendum to the portfolio specifying what additional information is required; or deny the petition for credit.

### TRANSCRIPTING THE CREDIT

Credit is transcripted on a course-by-course basis in a separate area of the transcript entitled "Credit Earned through Portfolio." Only passing portfolio credit is recorded. A typical transcription would read: COM 310 Interpersonal Communication 3.00 credits.

### PORTFOLIO FEES

There is no separate portfolio application fee. The cost for the ED 202 course is the current established tuition for either classroom or online coursework.

The portfolio fee is based on the number of credits to be assessed and is non-refundable if the portfolio is not approved. Assessors are paid per the credits petitioned by the student.

## USE OF TECHNOLOGY IN THE PORTFOLIO PROCESS

Technology is used throughout the portfolio process. The ED 202 course is available in an online format with a supporting website for the course (*http://academic.regis.edu/ed202*). Students are expected to be able to use Microsoft Word for essay submission, research the Internet for appropriate course descriptions that match their learning, and submit their portfolios electronically using iWebfolio software. Part of the portfolio includes documentation that may need to be scanned.

Other uses of technology include the following:

◆ Use the Internet to research possible course descriptions that match the student's learning

◆ Access the supporting website for the portfolio course (*http://academic. regis.edu/ed202*)

◆ The online course is on ANGEL LMS platform

◆ The portfolio is submitted and reviewed by faculty using iWebfolio software (*www.iwebfolio.com*)

◆ Documents in the portfolio use a variety of formats (e.g., Word, PowerPoint, Excel, jpeg, pdf, video, audio, etc.)

# REGIS UNIVERSITY STATISTICAL PROFILE: 2006–2007

a. Total number of credits reviewed by portfolio assessment in the last academic year (Fall through Summer sessions of the academic year) 2006–2007: 840

b. Average number of credits awarded based upon all students receiving "portfolio-awarded" credits during the academic year 2006–2007: 810

c. Total number of students at the institution during the academic year 2006–2007: 16,000 (Regis University total); 5,300 (College for Professional Studies Undergraduate; i.e., those able to participate in PLA programs)

d. Total number of the students at the institution who participated in the Portfolio Assessment Program during the academic year 2006–2007: 275

## *CD-ROM, REGIS UNIVERSITY: ITEMS 1A-F TO 4*

**CD-ROM**

1. Portfolio Sample COM 310 Interpersonal Communication
   a. Personal Learning Theme (Goals Oriented Autobiography)
   b. Web Advisor Transcript
   c. Course Description
   d. Portfolio Essay Summary (Reflecting Kolb's Experiential Learning Theory)
   e. Course Essay
   f. PLA Documentation Index and Documentation

2. PLA FAQs

3. Regis Prior Learning Assessment Department Policies and Procedures

4. Assessment Outcomes

**Spring Arbor, Michigan**

Founded by the abolitionist Free Methodist Church in the third-quarter of the nineteenth century, Spring Arbor University in south central Michigan is a church-affiliated institution that welcomes students of all faiths. It grew out of a seminary for elementary and secondary education, gaining a junior college in 1929. Eventually, the collegiate aspect outpaced the original seminary and by the early 1960s, the institution came to be known as Spring Arbor College. Accreditation by the North Central Association in 1960 was the impetus for rapid curricular growth. Now, in the first decade of the twenty-first century, Spring Arbor University continues to grow. Since 2000, Spring Arbor University has added 174,000 square feet and renovated an additional 69,000 square feet of facilities. Maturing from college to university status in 2001, Spring Arbor University has set enrollment records and balanced its $49 million operating budget every year. Both traditional undergraduate enrollment (1,570) and total enrollment (4,002) have increased over 40 percent.

## BRIEF HISTORY OF ADULT EDUCATION AT SPRING ARBOR

Beginning in the 1980s, Spring Arbor University served adult learners through a degree completion program based in nearby Jackson, Michigan. Branching out from its initial offering of a bachelor's degree in Human Resource Management, the adult education program soon added majors in health careers. Spring Arbor developed a consortium of twenty colleges and universities that act as affiliates for the School of Adult Studies. This adult-centered program currently has thirteen sites in Michigan and Ohio, with program choices ranging from business to human services to teacher education, with some sites offering certification.

In order to enroll, adult learners must have fifty-eight semester hours from an accredited institution(s). These can include prior learning assessment (PLA) credits. The new Associate of Arts degree in the School of Adult Studies allows prospective bachelor's degree students with less than fifty-eight credits an in-house option for meeting the admission requirement while being able to develop an early focus on their projected four-year degree.

## PRIOR LEARNING ASSESSMENT AT SPRING ARBOR UNIVERSITY

Prior learning assessment has long been available to all Spring Arbor students, but it was more rapidly embraced by adult learners. When Spring Arbor University began offering its first degree completion program in 1983, a requirement was the completion of a two-credit module called "Career Assessment and Planning" in which students completed a portfolio notebook. This course included instruction on submitting professional development training [see Items 3 and 4, *Professional Schools and Training (PSTs)*, and Item 8, *Writing a Life-Learning Paper (LLP)*, a handbook for students, on the CD-ROM]. Each student was required to (1) write five life-learning papers (this was changed twice; the current requirement is three papers); (2) compile all professional training as part a notebook submission; and (3) include a résumé, an autobiography, and copies of the student's transcripts. Students could earn up to thirty credits from the evaluation of this portfolio. Those credits were the primary way for students to earn credits above and beyond what transferred credits and credits earned in the program, thus allowing them to reach the total number of credits needed for graduation more quickly. Additional PSTs and LLPs could be submitted for evaluation subsequent to the evaluation of the portfolio notebook. (See Items 2, 5, 6, and 7 on the CD-ROM.)

In 1988, the portfolio requirement was moved to Module 1 of the program as part of a four-credit class called "Adult Development and Life Planning." This course was team-taught by an assessment counselor who provided portfolio instruction and a faculty member who taught adult development theory. Students were required to produce a portfolio notebook that included the same components as previously, including the two PLA components (PSTs and LLPs), but the student had to include only one LLP as part of the portfolio (see Item 1, *Portfolio Sample, LLP* on the CD-ROM). Subsequent papers could be submitted throughout the program as part of the student's overall academic plan. In this iteration, the portfolio was graded for 40 percent of the module grade.

In 1998, a major curriculum revision resulted in the first module being a three-credit course on Adult Development, and the second module a two-credit course on writing. The final product of the writing course was a single LLP that the student could then submit separately for evaluation for credit—the "portfolio" was no longer the vehicle for prior learning credit. Instead, students' individual academic plans (IAP) included appropriate LLPs and PSTs, each to be submitted and evaluated on their own. Professional Schools and Training instruction, which had previously been done by the assessment counselor, was now provided via a booklet which was presented to students by their academic advisors (see Items 3 and 4 on the CD-ROM). For many students, writing LLPs continued to be their best option for earning at least some of their IAP credits.

As part of this revision process, the portfolio was eliminated from the assessment for prior learning and, instead, became an exit piece prepared by selected cohort groups and submitted to area business people for assessment of the entire program. These evaluators then compared the portfolio contents with the published learning objectives for the program. Consequently, the organizational culture of the program was modified—the terms "portfolio credits" or credits "earned in portfolio" were no longer used; instead referring to "PLA credits" or "IAP credits."

Including LLP instruction in the writing module continued until 2005 when a major revision in the writing curriculum removed LLP instruction from the module. As the numbers of students in their twenties increased, it became obvious that writing even one paper was difficult for most of those younger students. Students now had lots of other options for earning the required number of graduation credits: increased weekend college offerings at Spring Arbor University, more online classes at Spring Arbor and other Michigan institutions, and more student-friendly schedules at local community colleges. So the role of the LLP as the primary way to earn those credits had changed. Currently, the LLP, free to students, is available for those who wish to include LLPs in their individual academic plans.

Prior learning assessment is an option that has always been open to main campus students as well as to Adult Studies students. Over the years, the participation in this option by non-traditional (older than 18–22 years) main campus students has increased. Some departments recommend this option more than others, but PLA is obviously a great option for older students returning to school, even in a traditional program with a traditional delivery system.

With the advent of several graduate programs at Spring Arbor University, provisions for prior learning at the graduate level have been included as well. Most of the time students submit professional training to be evaluated, but there has been one LLP that earned credit even at the graduate level.

# THE PLA PROGRAM AT SPRING ARBOR

## *LEARNING ABOUT THE PLA PROGRAM*

Spring Arbor University adult studies students learn about the general concept of PLA during pre-program recruitment and advising. The admissions person looks very generally at options for each student, and the academic advisor helps the student identify more specifically what training they might submit or what LLP topics might be appropriate, a determination based on the student's academic needs in coordination with the student's experiences and potential for learning from those experiences.

Main campus and graduate students learn about PLA options from their faculty advisors or from academic advising venues like the Registrar's office. These students come to the PLA office for further information and training in preparing their credit submissions.

## Participation Requirements and Limitations

Students must be enrolled at Spring Arbor University to qualify for submitting prior learning credit requests. Students can count up to thirty PLA credits toward graduation. Except where limited by accreditation of certain programs (e.g., nursing and social work), students may use PLA for general education requirements or for elective credits, or, as long as they are meeting departmental requirements, for credits toward their majors/minors. The only limitations are that students have the experience base, that the PLA is not duplicating any other course work, and that the learning is college level. Students are not restricted to content areas that are offered only at Spring Arbor University. If the content is college level anywhere, students will be allowed to document and submit those experiences, the rationale being that transfer courses are routinely accepted in curriculum areas that are not offered at Spring Arbor.

## Assessment Practices

A variety of people evaluate the LLPs. Most are either current or former faculty, either from our main campus site or our off-campus sites around Michigan. To be a regular evaluator, individuals must submit transcripts to the appropriate departments to be approved as evaluators in certain topic areas. However, individuals in the community who are experts in certain topics are used on occasion. Anyone who evaluates LLPs is trained before he/she does an evaluation. (see Item 9, *Evaluator Rubric*; Item 10, *Evaluator Training Handbook*; and Item 11, *Training on the Rubric for LLP Evaluators, PowerPoint*; on the CD-ROM).

Evaluators are expected to have read papers within two weeks of receiving them. If an evaluator keeps a paper longer than three weeks, a reminder is sent.

## Student Preparation for PLA

Students who write LLPs attend a required LLP workshop. No credit is granted for attending the workshop; it is free to students, usually offered in a four-hour block on a Friday night or a Saturday. Workshops are offered around the state by Spring Arbor faculty throughout the year so that students who wish to write LLPs have several opportunities to attend. There is a standardized curriculum for the workshop. Figure 1 entitled the LLP Trail Flow Chart delineates the process.

Students who submit PSTs for their professional training receive a booklet that includes instruction on documentation and techniques to ensure that the write-up articulates learning outcomes and application. These students work with their advisors on this documentation/submission process.

Main campus students may attend an LLP workshop in a nearby off-campus site, but usually they come to the PLA office to receive one-on-one training. An on-line workshop is planned for the future.

## Faculty

The LLP workshops are taught by writing specialists who teach the writing modules in the degree completion programs. The workshops are not a part of

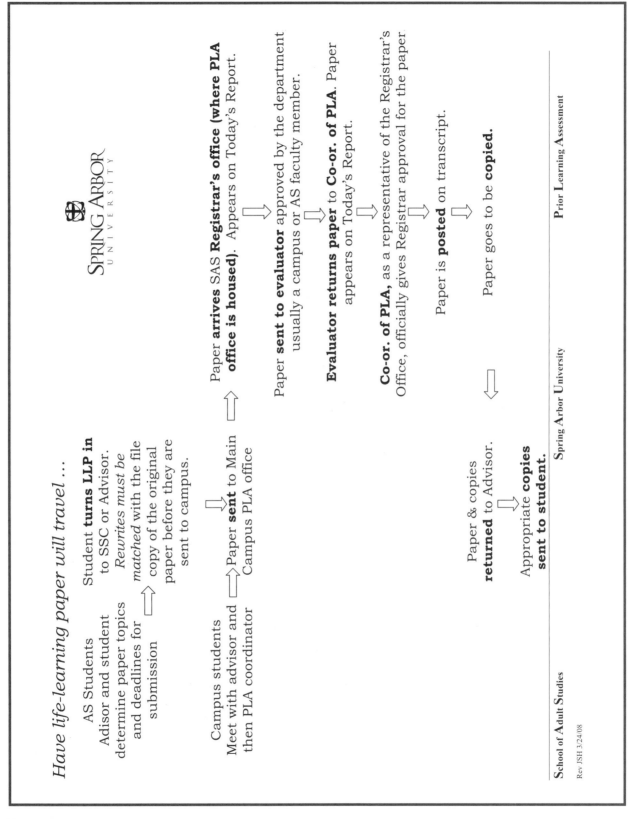

*Have life-learning paper will travel …*

**AS Students**
Adisor and student determine paper topics and deadlines for submission

Student **turns LLP in** to SSC or Advisor. *Rewrites must be matched* with the file copy of the original paper before they are sent to campus.

Campus students
Meet with advisor and then PLA coordinator

Paper **sent** to Main Campus PLA office

**SPRING ARBOR**
U N I V E R S I T Y

Paper **arrives** SAS **Registrar's office (where PLA office is housed).** Appears on Today's Report.

Paper **sent to evaluator** approved by the department usually a campus or AS faculty member.

**Evaluator returns paper** to **Co-or. of PLA**. Paper appears on Today's Report.

**Co-or. of PLA,** as a representative of the Registrar's Office, officially gives Registrar approval for the paper

Paper is **posted** on transcript.

Paper goes to be **copied.**

Paper & copies **returned** to Advisor.

Appropriate **copies sent to student.**

**School of Adult Studies**

Rev JSH 3/24/08

Spring Arbor University

Prior Learning Assessment

**FIGURE 1** ◆ LLP Trail Flow Chart

their regular faculty load, so they are paid separately for teaching them. In addition, they are paid for reviewing one LLP per workshop participant prior to the student's submitting the paper for credit. Only some students take advantage of this feedback opportunity.

### Credit Awards for Life-Learning Papers

Life-learning papers and PSTs are not graded but are awarded credit on a credit/no credit basis. The expectation, though, is that these submissions are prepared in such a way that they would receive a "C" or better if they were graded, so nothing gets credit that is not at least at a "C" level. This distinction is important for students who may need to transfer prior learning credit later, or who hope to get reimbursed by their employers for classes that are "C" or above. The rather extensive rubric used by Spring Arbor for the LLPs helps evaluators objectify some of these "C" characteristics.

Credit is transcripted primarily in a course-match format. Anyone looking at the transcript should be able to determine the general content of the prior learning credit, and thus be able to guard against duplication of credit for the same content at a later date.

Life-learning papers usually earn two to four credits and are titled appropriately on the transcript; for example, Marriage and Family, Spiritual Growth and Development, Psychology of Adjustment. Life-learning papers are designated LL on the transcript in the "grade" column. Life-learning credit is posted in the appropriate discipline but with a generic course number, as 295 for lower level credit, 395 for upper level credit, or 595 for graduate level credit (e.g., SOC295, BUS395, GES295, EDU595).

Professional schools and training credits are transcripted the same way, with a course designation, but there may be certain "block credit" elements to these postings. For example, training from the Michigan Fire Fighter's Training Council could earn up to 15 credits for Firefighter I and Firefighter II levels, and they would not typically be broken down into smaller elements such as Hazardous Materials or First Aid. Professional schools and training credit is designated as PR in the "grade" column of the transcript and had the generic course numbers 296, 396, and 596.

### Fees Related to Prior Learning Assessment

There is no charge for the LLP workshop or for posting credits to a student's transcript. Instead, an assessment fee is charged, designed primarily to offset the cost of evaluation. This PLA fee is based on the number of credits the student requests, not on the number of credits he/she earns.

A student meets with his or her academic advisor (week 12 of the program) to formalize the individual academic plan (IAP) for completing all graduation requirements. The advisor estimates the PLA fee for that student based on the number of PLA credits in the plan, and his/her account is charged at that time. This fee is charged only once for each paper, that is, students can submit rewrites without paying an additional fee. Once the paper has been evaluated, however, the student must pay the fee, regardless of whether or not the credit is earned. The fee is reviewed upon completion of the academic program; if more or less PLA credits are received than originally planned, an adjustment can be made at that time. Students can also request that an adjustment be made earlier if they wish.

On-campus students and graduate students either submit payment at the time they submit their LLPs/PSTs, or they have the charges added to their accounts. When the PLA office receives one of these papers, the appropriate officer sends a journal entry to the business office so the student's account can be charged.

Currently, undergraduate students pay $30 per credit assessed up to 10, $300 for 10–19 credits assessed, and $600 for 20–30 credits assessed. Graduate students pay $150 for the first 1 or 2 credits assessed and $75 per additional credit assessed after that. Evaluators currently are paid $35 to read an original LLP, $20 to read an LLP rewrite, $13 to read an undergraduate PST, $75 to read a graduate PST, and $25 to read a rewrite of a graduate PST.

## TECHNOLOGY IN THE PLA PROGRAM

Spring Arbor staff have designed a program in Microsoft Access for tracking all prior learning assessment activity. This program not only keeps track of the evaluators and when the papers were sent to them, but it also generates a note to students when papers arrive in the Adult Education office. Additionally, it summarizes monthly payroll information and generates reports that are then sent to the payroll office. As well, the program allows the Adult Education office to generate a Word document showing all the PLA activity on a daily basis, a report that is emailed to all the advisors throughout the state.

The staff is currently in the process of configuring the LLP workshop as a course in Blackboard so that on-line students from outside Michigan will have better access to LLP instruction. Life-learning paper forms are available to the students on "MySAU portal," and papers are occasionally submitted electronically, although evaluation is almost always done via hard copy.

One very low-tech element of the PLA program at Spring Arbor is distinctly printed inter-office envelopes that are dedicated to PLA use only. That way, when a LLP lands in a professor's mailbox, he/she can immediately identify it as a time-sensitive item.

## SPRING ARBOR UNIVERSITY STATISTICAL PROFILE: 2006–2007

a. Total number of credits reviewed by portfolio assessment in the last academic year (Fall through Summer sessions of the academic year) 2006–2007: 945

b. Average number of credits awarded based upon all students receiving "portfolio-awarded" credits during the academic year 2006–2007:

◆ Since our students submit individual learning experiences, the averages reflect that most students who submit, earn 1–3 credits through PLA

◆ Average number of credits awarded per student who submitted individual learning experiences: 2.19

◆ Average number of credits awarded per individual submission: 1.56
   —604 submissions
   —945 credits awarded
   —432 students who submitted

c. Total number of students at the institution during the academic year 2006–2007: 3,713

◆ Adult Studies and External Teacher Education programs (undergraduate): 1,038

◆ Main campus (undergraduate): 1,570

◆ Graduate: 1,105

d. Total number of the students at the institution who participated in the Portfolio Assessment Program during the academic year 2006–2007: 432

◆ Total number of credits awarded by PLA: 945

◆ Average number of credits awarded per student who submitted: 2.19

◆ Average number of credits awarded per submission: 1.56
   —604 submissions
   —945 credits awarded
   —432 students who submitted

**CD-ROM**

### *CD-ROM Spring Arbor University: Items 1 to 12*

1. Portfolio Sample: (Life-Learning Paper) WRT 312 Critical Analysis and Research Writing

2. Why Offer PLA?

3. Professional Schools and Training (PST) Handbook, edited

4. PST Handout for Students, Assessment Information

5. Life-Learning Experience Paper Guideline, Health Issues

6. Life-Learning Experience Paper Guideline, Psychology of Adjustment

7. Life-Learning Experience Paper Guideline, Marriage and Family

8. Writing a Life-Learning Paper (a handbook for students)

9. Evaluator Rubric (for Assessing Life-Learning Papers)

10. Evaluator Training Handbook

11. Training on the Rubric for LLP Evaluators, PowerPoint

12. Assessment Outcomes

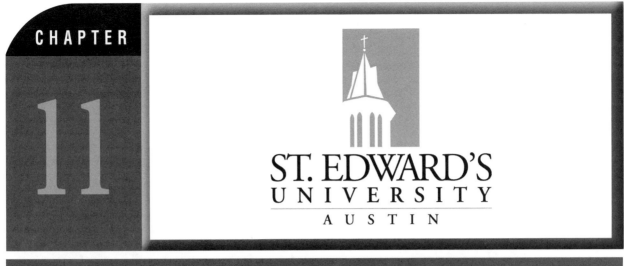

CHAPTER

11

ST. EDWARD'S
UNIVERSITY
AUSTIN

Austin, Texas

From inauspicious beginnings as a bequeathment to the Roman Catholic Congregation of the Holy Cross in Austin, Texas, St. Edward's Academy opened in 1878 with just three farm boys as its inaugural class. After becoming a university in 1925, St. Edward's went on to offer a liberal arts education, remaining a young men's university. A major shift would take place in the post-World War II decade when many of St. Edward's incoming students would be adult veterans attending college on the G.I. Bill. This was the beginning of St. Edward's long association with adult education.

With the massive social changes of the 1960s, St. Edward's would change again, admitting women from its "sister" institution, Maryhill College. The year was 1966; within four short years, "co-education" would become so mainstream that Maryhill ceased to exist as a separate entity and the female students formally joined their male cohort at St. Edward's. Just as the G.I. Bill had changed the face of St. Edward's following the Second World War, enrollment by Vietnam veterans entailed a new surge of adult students. In 1974, St. Edward's established the New College, a program centered on adult learners ages 24 and up (or with a minimum of five years work experience). It was spearheaded by Dr. Jean Meyer (Immaculate Heart of Mary), who went on to serve as New College Dean for nearly a decade.

The now thousands of successful graduates attest to the institution's effectiveness at meeting the needs of the adult student. Writing about innovative adult-oriented programs, Maehl (1999) touted St. Edward's New College as a premier institution for adult education.

Offering a variety of instructional options, New College awards the Bachelor of Arts, Bachelor of Business Administration, and Bachelor of Liberal Studies degrees. Students can opt for traditional majors or custom-tailor a degree program with the guidance of the enthusiastic faculty. Coursework is offered in the evening/weekend model, through one-on-one directed study, with the traditional daytime classroom-base, on-line, and in hybrid courses.

## PRIOR LEARNING ASSESSMENT

Prior learning portfolio assessment is also open to adult learners, in which documentation of skills learned and applied outside the classroom leads to college credit. "The Center for Prior Learning Assessment (CPLA) assists New College students with advising, instruction and coordination of the assessment of student portfolios, a way to individually assess the work experience and prior learning of adult students for possible college credit" (http://www.stedwards.edu/newc/current/services.htm).

## ELIGIBILITY AND ACCESS

The portfolio option benefits adult students in a wide variety of ways. In addition to receiving credit for work already done through career, avocation, or military service, students pay a lower fee for the inclusion of those assessed credits (at present, $67 per credit hour). The credits count toward degree requirements but they are ungraded, thus not factoring into the mature student's GPA. The reflection and documentation processes inherent in portfolio preparation help the adult learner engage in successful résumé writing, focus on potential paths for career enhancement, and be better prepared to present diverse skills to a potential new employer in the event of an unexpected career change.

## ASSESSMENT PRACTICES

All New College students wishing to take advantage of prior learning assessment are required to take a one-credit Prior Learning Assessment Seminar (PLAS). There they learn how to translate Adult Learning Theory into an applied exercise in self-assessment, shepherding one course request through the entire process, while gaining an advisor, namely the faculty member leading the seminar. After successful completion of the PLAS, adult learners have one academic year to prepare and submit all requests for prior learning credit. (Exceptions, including extensions, are possible).

Petitions are made as a single submission for each semester, but each of these submissions can contain requests for awarding of credit in lieu of several existing courses.

PLA seekers are not permitted to discuss the contents of submitted requests with the advisor unless the advisor initiates a request for clarification. Likewise, such students must not register for a "real" course equivalent to the PLA request under consideration. While adult learners can successfully navigate a degree program at New College without prior learning assessment, if chosen, this three-semester process should not be postponed any later than the start of the academic year before "senior" year.

Prior learning assessment can make a significant contribution to an adult learner's progress at New College.

In summary, eligible students seeking credit for prior learning follow these steps:

1. The student submits a completed portfolio to the Center for Prior Learning Assessment.

2. The Director reviews the portfolio, checks the originality via *Turnitin.com* (learning essays have to be submitted to *turnitin.com*), and notifies Student Financial Services for billing purposes.

3. CPLA staff enter the submission into a database.

4. The Director assigns and notifies the evaluator, sending the assessment form via email.

5. The Evaluator picks up the binder (at least until the e-portfolio is fully deployed) and reviews the portfolio.

   a. If the portfolio receives credit or is denied outright, the binder is returned to the CPLA along with a print-out of the evaluation form with the evaluator's hand signature and date.

   b. If the Evaluator requests additional documentation, the Director notifies the student, who then has three weeks to provide the materials requested. If the student fails to do so, the portfolio is denied. If the documentation is provided, the assessment process resumes at point 5a.

6. All assessment results are reviewed by the CPLA Director and the Dean.

   a. If assessment results are approved, proceed to point 7.

   b. If an internal re-assessment is requested, the process returns to point 4 and a new Evaluator is assigned to do a blind reassessment.

7. Assessment results go to the Registrar for processing and entry on the transcript. Copies of the evaluation form are scanned into the student's record. At the same time, assessment results are mailed to the student.

   a. If the student is satisfied with the outcome, the process is ended.

   b. If the student wishes to appeal the results the CPLA Director is first consulted and then the Dean is formally petitioned. If the Dean allows the appeal to proceed, a new Evaluator is assigned to perform a blind reassessment of the same materials seen by the original Evaluator. The judgment of the second Evaluator is considered final and there is no further appeal.

(See Items 1, 2, and 3 on the CD-ROM: *Portfolio Sample, Portfolio Advertising Documents,* and *Portfolio: Frequently Asked Questions.*)

St. Edward's accepts transfer credits from other regionally accredited institutions, and students may also receive credit through proficiency examinations (CLEP, DANTES, or by "challenging" tests in existing courses). A certificated learning program is another innovation, assessing academic credit for non-academic licenses and certificates such as those for real estate agents.

Dr. Susan C. Gunn, Director of the CPLA, orients new faculty in one-on-one training re experiential learning assessment. On a regular basis, she assembles faculty in designated instructional areas to ensure that all are assessing prior learning with the same, consistent standards.

## COMPENSATION OF PORTFOLIO EVALUATORS

New College contract faculty are required to perform assessments as part of their work load and receive no additional compensation. This is a significant concern among some faculty, because evaluators in areas such as computer science or communications perform many more assessments than those in disciplines like anthropology or history. At this time, there is no monetary compensation for this service. The program director attempts to equally distribute assessments in frequently requested areas by including traditional St. Edward's University faculty.

Contract faculty in St. Edward's traditional program are compensated at $30 per clock hour, as are adjunct faculty and community experts. This rate has not changed since 1999, and recent budget cuts across the university make the possibility of a raise very remote. In no way whatsoever are faculty compensated in terms of hours granted; we believe that such a compensation system would impugn the integrity of the assessment process by creating an incentive for faculty to award credit for substandard submissions.

## USE OF TECHNOLOGY IN ASSESSMENT

Our assessment forms are distributed to faculty assessors via email as file attachments. As of March 2008, iWebfolio software is being piloted for e-folios. Most sections of the Prior Learning Assessment Seminar (portfolio prep class) use Blackboard. Without a web presence, we distribute syllabi, portfolio forms, and other resources to students via email for the most part.

## ST. EDWARD'S UNIVERSITY STATISTICAL PROFILE: 2006–2007

a. Total number of credits reviewed by portfolio assessment in the last academic year (Fall through Summer sessions of the academic year) 2006–2007: 836

b. Average number of credits awarded based upon all students receiving "portfolio-awarded" credits during the academic year 2006–2007: 6

c. Total number of students at the institution during the academic year 2006–2007: 4,900 (941 of these are adults enrolled in New College)

d. Total number of the students at the institution who participated in the Portfolio Assessment Program during the academic year 2006–2007: 141

### CD-ROM, ST. EDWARD'S UNIVERSITY: ITEMS 1 TO 4

**CD-ROM**

1. Portfolio Sample: Arts Administration I
2. Portfolio Advertising Documents 1 and 2
3. Portfolio: Frequently Asked Questions
4. Assessment Outcomes

# St. Joseph's College
## NEW YORK

**1916**

## Brooklyn, New York

From its inception in 1974, the [then] Division of General Studies and [now], the School of Professional and Graduate Studies (PGS) has operated on the assumption that the college-level experiential learning of adults is an asset that can be translated into academic credit, which can be applied toward completing the requirements of the baccalaureate degree (Thomas G. Travis' Alliance/ACE Conference paper as cited in the Student Handbook, Portfolio and Career Development Seminar, Spring, 2008, p.1).

Adults bring to the college experience a wide array of talents and expertise, some of it from a traditional collegiate program, and some of it from non-traditional sources, such as professional training programs, . . . certificate programs, and . . . from their own work experience. What makes . . . PGS unique . . . is the ability to consider all these sources ("Transfer or Experiential Credit," http://www.sjcny.edu/printpage.php/prmID/286).

St. Joseph's College is accredited by the Commission on Higher Education, Middle States Association of Colleges and Schools and is registered with the New York State Education Department ("Accreditations," http://www.sjcny.edu/page.php/prmID/17).

## PRIOR LEARNING ASSESSMENT

St. Joseph's College recognizes that adults who begin degree programs bring knowledge and skills acquired through a variety of modes. Within PGS, the award of credit may be determined through:

◆ Collegiate coursework

◆ Non-collegiate sponsored instruction

◆ Proficiency examinations

◆ Prior experiential learning assessment [Portfolio] (*Student Handbook*, 2008, p. 6).

The School of Professional and Graduate Studies students, except for Nursing majors, with extensive and varied experiential learning may participate in the Prior Experiential Learning Assessment (P.E.L.A.) Program . . . Validated learning, not experience alone is the basis for awarding credit. Students must be matriculated, have satisfactorily completed ENG 103 Writing for Effective Communication and have earned 36 credits toward their program at St. Joseph's or elsewhere. Students in all majors except Nursing are eligible for portfolio assessment (*2007/2009 Catalogue*, http://www.sjcny.edu/media/2615_PGSCourseCatalogueBothopt.pdf, pp. 15–18).

In addition, suitability for portfolio assessment requires that students have a satisfactory cumulative grade point average, and meet with the P.E.L.A. Coordinator/advisor to receive permission to register for the required three-credit, GS110 Portfolio and Career Development Seminar.

The course provides the necessary principles to prepare an experiential portfolio through individualized exercises that help the student identify acquired skills and competencies, and relating these to coursework and career goals. This mentored course of approximately twelve to fifteen students is required of all students seeking prior experiential learning assessment credit. Students must take the Seminar before their last semester. In addition, an integral part of the Seminar is the validation process, which consists of assembling all relevant credentials into the portfolio document under the supervision of a qualified mentor. Portfolios are evaluated by faculty members, and a credit award is made by the P.E.L.A. Evaluation Committee, taking into consideration the content, competence level, college credit appropriateness, and applicability to the student's degree program. Notification of the credit award is sent to the students by the Registrar prior to the conclusion of the next regular semester (Item 2, *Student Handbook*, St. Joseph's College New York, pp. 1–54 on the CD-ROM). Because the student is under the direct tutelage of an experienced mentor, there is less likelihood of the need for appeal regarding the credit award, though a policy exists should the need arise (*2007/2009 PGS Catalogue*, pp. 15–18).

Credit earned through the P.E.L.A. Program may be applied to the major, liberal arts requirements, and electives. In certain degrees (that is, Bachelor of Science in Community Health and Human Services and/or Organizational Management), there are specific policies regarding the placement of credits earned. A maximum of twenty-seven credits may be awarded via the P.E.L.A. Program (*2007/2009 PGS Catalogue*, p. 17; L. Fonte, personal communication, July 18, 2008).

Students learn of the P.E.L.A. Program at new student orientation, in individual academic advisement sessions, from the college's website, and through informational prior learning workshops. There are two P.E.L.A. faculty at the Long Island campus (one is the Coordinator and the other the online Seminar faculty) and one Coordinator in Brooklyn. A faculty from English or Counseling may also teach the Seminar in Brooklyn. When a student meets with the Coordinator, the student receives the Application and Registration Procedures (see Item 3, on the CD-ROM). The course, GS 110 Portfolio and Career Development Seminar, is offered both face-to-face and online. This mentored course affords adult learners the opportunity to "identify college level learning, based on professional experience, such as management, supervision, marketing, quality improvement, community service, etc. The learning demonstrated is more closely allied with a 'discipline-centered' approach to assessment rather than a course equivalency model" (L. Fonte, personal communication, July 18, 2008). All elements of the portfolio are completed within the framework of the course. In rare instances, a "no credit option" is offered where a student may work independently with a mentor to prepare the portfolio without enrolling or receiving credit in the portfolio course. There is no grade for either the course or the portfolio. Credit is recorded as "PEL," either 100 levels (for lower division learning) or 300 levels (for upper division learning).

Fees include the regular three-credit tuition for an undergraduate course, and a $250 assessment fee payable upon registration for the course (for either the course or the "no credit option"). The assessment fees provide the monies to subsidize the faculty evaluator's compensation. There is no posting fee.

## ASSESSMENT PRACTICES

The *Student Handbook 2007/2009* outlines in great detail the philosophy, policies, and practices for portfolio development. This document is distributed as part of the Seminar that provides the context for students to complete their portfolio documents. Final portfolios are forwarded to the P.E.L.A. Coordinator by the course mentor with appropriate comments. The Coordinator reviews the portfolios with two purposes: "(a) an initial overview assessment of each petition addressing the issues of credit requested, duplication, policy violations, and overall quality, and (b) the distribution of the individual petitions to the appropriate subject matter/academic experts" (*Student Handbook*, p. 52). The assigned faculty expert then makes the credit award recommendation (see Item 4, *Portfolio Assessment Policies for Evaluators,* on the CD-ROM). Full-time faculty are required to evaluate up to eight petitions per semester (where appropriate), and receive compensation for any beyond that number. They, as do adjuncts, receive the prevailing academic advisement rate, which is presently $28.00 per hour. Outside experts receive $50.00 per petition.

Figure 1 entitled Prior Experiential Learning Assessment Flow Chart delineates the portfolio process in greater detail and provides all participants with information to ensure consistency in prior learning credit evaluation.

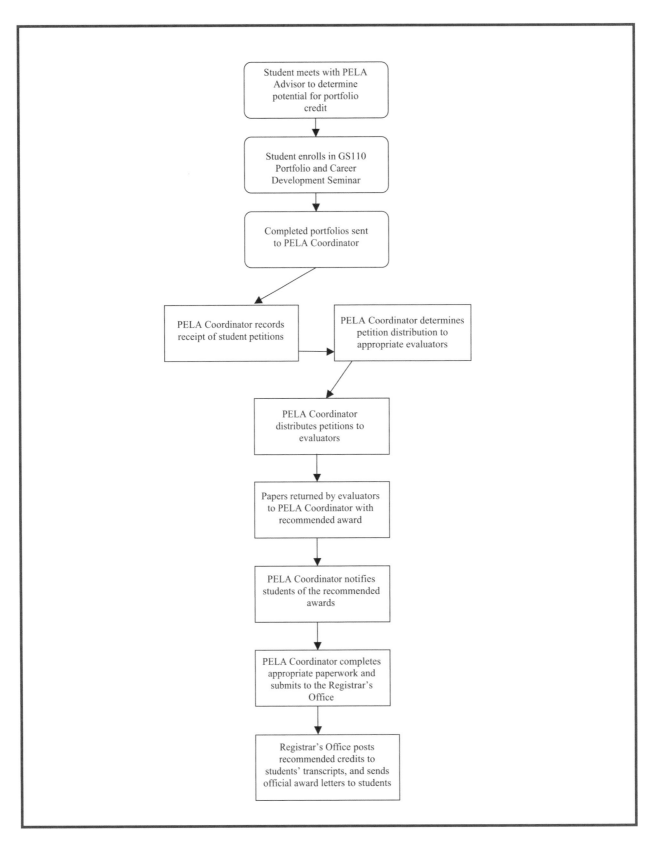

**FIGURE 1** ◆ PLA Process Flow Chart

76        CHAPTER 12

## STUDENT PORTFOLIO PETITIONS

"Each (student portfolio) petition will consist of a resume, outline, typed petition, support and validation material, the Mentor Comment form, and the Subject Matter/Academic Expert Comments form. If there are special concerns, there may also be a note from the P.E.L.A.Coordinator" (see Item 4, *Portfolio Assessment Policies for Evaluators*, on the CD-ROM). The following questions as listed in the *Student Handbook* (p. 45) may be helpful for the student in drafting the petition:

◆ What have I learned?

◆ Where and when did this learning take place?

◆ Who helped me to learn?

◆ What was my responsibility and contribution to my group or committee?

◆ What duties did I perform?

◆ What responsibilities did I have?

◆ What activities was I involved in?

◆ What techniques and procedures did I master?

◆ What resources and equipment did I use?

◆ What training did I receive?

◆ What supplementary study, such as reading of books and articles, did I pursue?

The portfolio petition must fit within the student's degree program, must demonstrate college-level competencies, and must fulfill all requirements as outlined in the *Student Handbook* and other policies and procedures of the institution found in current college documents and the website regarding Prior Experiential Learning Assessment via Portfolio. A sample portfolio in the area of Facilities Administration is presented as Item 1 on the CD-ROM.

## USE OF TECHNOLOGY IN ASSESSMENT

In the course, GS 110 Portfolio and Career Development Seminar, mentors use email for student consultation, especially for papers, corrections, and comments. This seminar is conducted both face-to-face or online using the Blackboard platform.

a. Total number of credits reviewed by portfolio assessment in the last academic year (Fall through Summer sessions of the academic year) 2006–2007: 651

b. Average number of credits awarded based upon all students receiving "portfolio-awarded" credits during the academic year 2006–2007: 10

c. Total number of students at the institution during the academic year 2006–2007: Fall 2006: 1,277; Spring 2007: 1,175; Summer 2007: unavailable*

d. Total number of students at the institution who participated in the Portfolio Assessment Program during the academic year 2006–2007: 62

**CD-ROM**

### *CD-ROM, St. Joseph's College: Items 1 to 5*

1. Portfolio Sample: Facilities Administration

2. Student Handbook, Spring 2008

3. Registration Procedures and Application

4. Portfolio Assessment Policies for Evaluators

5. Assessment Outcomes

---

* Data are for the School of Professional and Graduate Studies undergraduate division for both campuses, Brooklyn and Long Island. The portfolio option does not apply to Arts and Sciences or Graduate students.

VALDOSTA
S T A T E
UNIVERSITY™

## Valdosta, Georgia

"The mission of Valdosta State University is to

◆ Prepare our students to meet global opportunities and challenges through excellence in teaching and learning.

◆ Expand the boundaries of current knowledge, and explore the practical applications of that knowledge, through excellence in scholarship and creative endeavors.

◆ Promote the economic, cultural, and educational progress of our community and of our region, through excellence in service outreach.

Valdosta State University seeks to accomplish this mission in a dynamic, student-centered learning environment marked by respect for the diverse abilities, backgrounds, and contributions of all members of the university community." (http://www.valdosta.edu/sra/documents/VSU_Concise_Mission.pdf)

Valdosta State University is accredited by the Commission on Colleges of the Southern Association of Colleges and Schools to award associate, bachelors, masters, educational specialist, and doctoral degrees. Numerous academic programs have attained accreditation from national professional organizations." (http://www.valdosta.edu/vsu/about/accreditation.shtml)

## BRIEF HISTORY OF PORTFOLIO ASSESSMENT AT VALDOSTA STATE UNIVERSITY

The Prior Learning Assessment (PLA) Program at Valdosta State University grew out of an initiative from the Board of Regents of the University System of Georgia and was funded by the Department of Education's Transition to Teaching grant. The original plan was to utilize PLA to recruit career-changers for teacher training programs in Georgia. Valdosta State University was selected to pilot a project that could be replicated at other University System of Georgia institutions. As planning progressed for the PLA Pilot Project, the decision was made to expand the program to other subject areas and majors beyond teacher training.

Planning for the PLA Pilot Project included administrators, faculty, and staff at Valdosta State University with significant guidance from a variety of sources within the state, from nationally recognized consultants, and from other experienced PLA Practitioners. During the planning period, a handbook was developed for students, faculty, staff, and administrators re the PLA program. This *Handbook* is framed by and adheres to the CAEL text *Assessing Learning* (Fiddler, Marienau, Whitaker, 2006).

Utilizing many of the assessment tools available, including the College-Level Examination Program (CLEP), Advanced Placement (AP), Defense Activity for Non-Traditional Educational Support (DANTES), American Council on Education (ACE), and existing departmental exams, Valdosta State University attempts to find an evaluation strategy that meets the student's needs, depending on the type of experiential learning, training, work experience, and other factors. If none of the established standardized methods fit the needs of the student, the student will then be advised to consider the possibilities of portfolio assessment to earn credit.

## ESTABLISHING SUPPORT AND DIRECTION

Two members of the Valdosta State University faculty visited another institution to learn about their PLA program and returned with a portfolio evaluation template. That template was adapted to be used by faculty assessors at Valdosta State University and a rubric system was developed for scoring the portfolios. Using the evaluation template model, assessment methods were initially established for courses in education, mathematics, and science.

The deans of each college were contacted to familiarize them with PLA practices and to seek their involvement in establishing courses that could be evaluated by portfolio. With the approval of the deans, presentations were made to department heads requesting that they designate courses for which students could earn credit through portfolio assessment. In those colleges and departments that agreed to consider granting PLA credit, members of the faculty were identified to participate in assessor training.

In the Spring and Summer semesters of 2008, the first students and faculty assessors were recruited to take part in the PLA Pilot Study. Training for faculty assessors occurred in February of 2008. Following the training, the faculty began working to identify courses in their departments eligible for PLA credit. Using the course outcomes, faculty assessors established appropriate evaluation templates. Rubrics were created for a total of twenty-seven courses in eleven subject areas by the end of May 2008 (see Item 3, *PERS 2730 Rubric;* Item 5, *NURS 4060 Rubric;* Item 8, *Prior Learning Assessment Resources* on the CD-ROM). Numerous other materials have been developed to assist all Valdosta State University faculty, staff, and administration personnel as they acclimate to the PLA Program. One such example is *The Role of Faculty Assessors,* Item 7 on the CD-Rom, brief FAQs for PLA Assessors. For many of the twenty-seven courses, PLA credit is demonstrated via portfolio assessment, employing a combination of documentation methods, essays, presentations, plus oral and written examinations. The first portfolios were reviewed during the Summer term of 2008 resulting in earned credit for a total of eleven courses representing four students. (See Items 2 and 4, both *Sample Portfolios,* on the CD-ROM.) At the time of this report some students were still working on portfolios and, in some cases, their work was in the process of being evaluated for possible credit.

## ELIGIBILITY AND ACCESS

Students are made aware of PLA by email messages targeted at those students who are 24 years of age and older and/or referred by faculty advisors or professors of their current course. The students who seek information on PLA from any source are directed to the PLA Counselor, who does the initial screening and advises the students about the possible methods for earning credit. Students must be accepted by Valdosta State University to take part in the PLA Program. It is possible, however, for students to meet with the PLA Counselor for guidance before actually applying to Valdosta State University.

Those students who qualify for CLEP, AP, ACE, DANTES, or departmental exams will be directed to the appropriate areas for assistance with those methods. Students seeking credit through the portfolio development option must take a two-credit course entitled PLA 2000 Portfolio Development. Figure 1, PLA Flow Chart, depicts the process for the PLA Program.

At present, the portfolio option includes twenty-seven courses in eleven subject areas, plus other existing departmental exams and CLEP, AP, ACE, and DANTES. Using those alternatives, students earn credit in the core curriculum, including free electives, and/or in upper-division or graduate courses. There is no minimum GPA or age requirement for consideration for the PLA Program; however, colleges or departments may restrict eligibility based on these variables. There also is no residency requirement. Students may earn credit up to a maximum of thirty hours through PLA.

Students must complete the PLA 2000 Portfolio Documentation course by the end of their junior year (ninety hours or more of credit) and cannot seek credit during their senior year. Policies and procedures for both students and faculty can be found in the *PLA Handbook* (Item 6 on the CD-ROM) and online in either PDF or electronic interactive formats. Students in the PLA 2000 course should use the *Handbook* as a resource to develop their portfolio documents.

## PRIOR LEARNING ASSESSMENT PRACTICES

Students who are advised to seek credit by portfolio take the two-credit course, PLA 2000 Portfolio Development. This course carries institutional credit but does not apply to the required credit hours needed for graduation. The PLA 2000 course provides students with guidance on portfolio development and self-assessment. The specific activities in the course depend on the subject areas for which students are seeking credit. Students will often be required to write essays on their personal learning experiences that might serve as a basis for them to apply for credit. Students who need help with writing and other basic skill areas are referred to the Student Success Center (SSC) for tutoring, while those who need assistance with career planning will be referred to the Counseling Center.

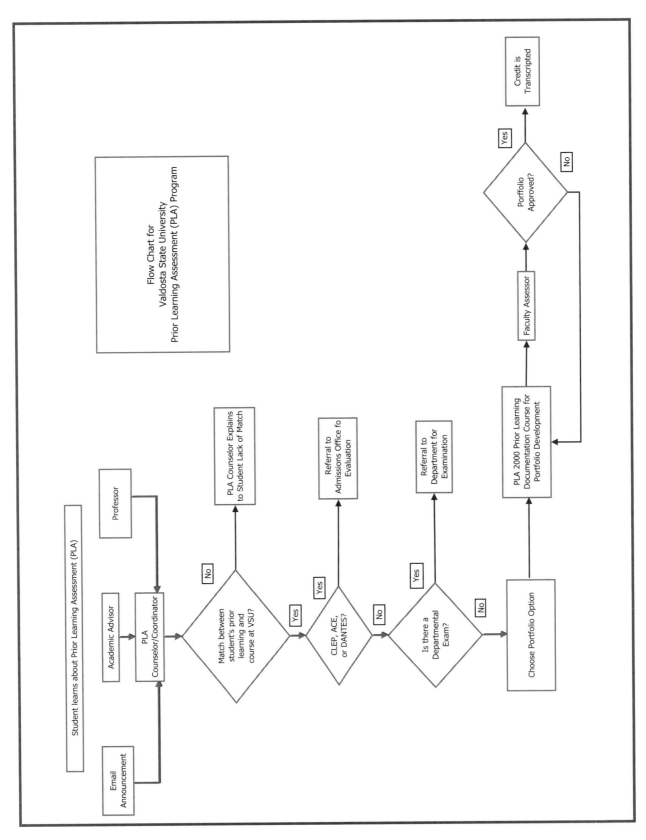

Flow Chart for
Valdosta State University
Prior Learning Assessment (PLA) Program

Student learns about Prior Learning Assessment (PLA)

Professor

Academic Advisor

Email Announcement

PLA Counselor/Coordinator

Match between student's prior learning and course at VSU?

No → PLA Counselor Explains to Student Lack of Match

Yes

CLEP, ACE, or DANTES?

Yes → Referral to Admissions Office fo Evaluation

No

Is there a Departmental Exam?

Yes → Referral to Department for Examination

No

Choose Portfolio Option

PLA 2000 Prior Learning Documentation Course for Portfolio Development

Faculty Assessor

Portfolio Approved?

Yes → Credit is Transcripted

No

**FIGURE 1** ◆ PLA Flow Chart

The PLA 2000 course may be graded as either satisfactory or unsatisfactory depending on the work submitted.

The PLA 2000 course, as part of the regular teaching load, is taught by a full-time faculty member who also serves as the PLA counselor. The PLA Counselor's assignment also includes recruiting faculty assessors, training assessors in evaluation methods, and serving as a liaison between the Valdosta State University administration, colleges, department heads, and faculty assessors.

Evaluation of a portfolio results in the determination by a faculty assessor of either a "satisfactory" or "unsatisfactory" assessment. "Satisfactory" performance is equivalent to the score of 70 or better. Faculty assessors may require specific, additional documentation and/or other work to be considered for a "satisfactory" score to be given as credit for the portfolio-assessed course. Items 2 and 4 on the CD-ROM are sample portfolios whereas Items 3 and 5 are sample associated rubrics. Credit earned through portfolio evaluation is transcripted based on a match with a specific VSU course. A sample entitled *Political Science Advising Checklist* notes the placement of portfolio awarded credit (see Item 2 on the CD-ROM).

Students who take the PLA 2000 course pay tuition by the credit hour at the same rate as other Valdosta State University courses. One portfolio evaluation is included with enrollment in the course. Subsequent portfolio reviews for credit will carry a fee of $50 per course evaluated.

At this time, all faculty assessors at Valdosta State University are full-time members of the faculty. The *PLA Handbook,* however, allows for others, including individuals in the community with expertise in a particular subject area to also serve as portfolio evaluators.

During the PLA Pilot Project, faculty assessors were compensated through a grant that funded the project. The compensation for evaluation efforts beyond that time is being considered.

Because the PLA Program is just in its early phase, it is likely that, through practice and reevaluation, changes are anticipated.

## THE USE OF TECHNOLOGY IN ASSESSMENT

The PLA 2000 Portfolio Development course is offered as an online course. Valdosta State University offers courses at several locations in addition to the main campus. By providing the PLA 2000 course on-line, it allows the university to provide instruction and assistance to students who might be at off-campus locations or who might need to work around existing course or work schedules. The students can meet with the instructor for assistance if necessary. The instructor remains in contact with students either face-to-face at off-campus locations, by phone, and/or by email.

Valdosta State University uses WebCT Vista courseware. Students submit all portfolio components in electronic file format through Vista and receive feedback with suggestions for revisions. The final product for each component is submitted in digital file format. The current requirement is for students to submit their *Application for Credit Through Prior Learning Assessment (PLA)* (Item 1 on the CD-ROM) and all components of the portfolio in Microsoft Office files or Adobe Acrobat (PDF) flies.

a. Total number of credits reviewed by portfolio assessment in the last academic year (Fall through Summer sessions of the academic year) 2006–2007:

   ◆ The Valdosta State University program was instituted as a pilot project in the 2007–2008 academic year. Therefore, all data represent that timeframe only. Academic year 2007–2008: 45

   NOTE: The assessment process included a combination of portfolio documentation plus oral and written exams, presentations, and other methods for most of the students who had evaluations completed.

b. Average number of credits awarded based upon all students receiving "portfolio-awarded" credits during the academic year 2007–2008: 10.5

c. Total number of students at the institution during the academic year 2007–2008: Approximately 11,000 students

d. Total number of the students at the institution who participated in the Portfolio Assessment Program during the academic year 2007–2008: 8 students (enrolled in PLA 2000 course)

   Other students have been screened and others have met with the PLA Counselor to determine creditable learning. Some of these students have also met with faculty assessors for further discussions about possible PLA credit. It is uncertain at this time if any of these students will sign up for the PLA 2000 course in Fall 2008 or later.

### ASSOCIATED WEBSITES

*http://www.valdosta.edu/pla/*

**CD-ROM**

### CD-ROM, VALDOSTA STATE UNIVERSITY: ITEMS 1 TO 9

1. Application for Credit through Prior Learning Assessment (PLA): PERS 2730 Internet Technology

2. Portfolio Sample: PERS 2730 Internet Technology

3. Rubric for Effective Prior Learning Assessment Submissions: PERS 2730 Internet Technology

4. Portfolio Sample: NURS 4060 Advanced Health Assessment

5. Rubric for Effective Prior Learning Assessment Submissions: NURS 4060 Advanced Health Assessment

6. Prior Learning Assessment (PLA) Program Handbook [Policies and Procedures for Students and Faculty]

7. The Role of Faculty Assessors [FAQs for PLA Assessors at Valdosta State University]

8. Prior Learning Assessment Resources [List of Courses Available via Portfolio Assessment]

9. Assessment Outcomes

VERMONT STATE COLLEGES

OFFICE OF EXTERNAL PROGRAMS

## Waterbury, Vermont

The Vermont State Colleges is a system of public colleges, created by act of the Vermont General Assembly in 1961. The five colleges in the system (and their founding dates) are Castleton State College (1787), Community College of Vermont (1970), Johnson State College (1828), Lyndon State College (1911), and the Vermont Technical College (1866). Together, these colleges enroll more than 13,000 students, more than 60 percent are from Vermont and about 40 percent are from forty other states and more than forty-five countries (Wikipedia, 2008).

Vermont's second largest and most affordable college, Community College of Vermont serves almost 9,500 students each year through twelve statewide learning sites and on-line. [Community College of Vermont] provides a quality, engaging educational experience to a diverse student population ranging in age from 16 to 80, from many cultures and backgrounds. With a dedicated faculty, who often work in the field they teach, and small, interactive classes, students are encouraged to share and learn from each other. Through convenient day, evening, weekend, online options, and courses that meet once a week, students have the flexibility to work and fulfill family obligations, while obtaining a first-rate education (http://www.vsc.edu/).

## PRIOR LEARNING ASSESSMENT IN THE VERMONT STATE COLLEGES

The Vermont State Colleges Assessment of Prior Learning (APL) Program is one of the oldest such programs in the country. Since 1975, nearly 6,000 students have received transfer credit through the program. The assessment process, which can take up to ten months, works in three steps:

1. After careful advising, students interested in and deemed good candidates for assessment of their prior, experiential learning enroll in a three-credit course offered through the Vermont State Colleges, usually at the statewide Community Colleges of Vermont due to the advantageous geographic distribution of the 12 Community Colleges of Vermont sites. The classes are, therefore, easily accessible to all Vermonters, and each of the twelve campuses offers the course either once or twice a year. The course is taught by specially selected and trained faculty. Students and faculty are supported extensively by the staff of the Vermont State Colleges Office of External Programs (OEP), which oversees and administers the process. The object of the class is the preparation of a portfolio that clearly and formally articulates and documents the student's learning. There is no limit to the number of credits a student can request and requests may fall into various areas of the curriculum.

2. At the end of the semester, all portfolios are submitted to OEP where they are extensively reviewed and grouped into content areas. Then four faculty members (and sometimes a qualified practitioner) are hired to pre-review a group of six to eight portfolios. Final decisions about credit awards are then made by a gathering of this group of reviewer/evaluators (an "Advanced Standing Committee"), which is chaired by the OEP Coordinator of Assessment Services. Decisions are made by consensus. The committee can make changes to the student requests and award or not award credit. The evaluation process is based on standards established by the Council for Adult and Experiential Learning (CAEL). Awarded credit is not institutional credit, but transfer credit. (In this, the Vermont program differs from programs that award credits for use within a specific institution.)

3. After the meeting of the Advanced Standing Committee, staff prepares and sends the student a transcript with all credits awarded from OEP/Vermont State Colleges. Finally, the student transfers this transcript to one of the five state colleges or another school of their choice that will accept experiential learning credit. The Office of External Programs itself does not award or offer any degrees; it simply handles the evaluation process of experiential learning for any Vermonter interested in such an assessment. Ninety-five percent of all "APL graduates" continue their education and transfer their awarded credits to a college as part of a degree plan.

The portfolio assessment program (APL) at Vermont State Colleges began in 1975. It is administered via a side arm of the five state colleges and is available to any Vermonter. Portfolio preparation is the largest aspect of the program, which also administers CLEP tests for the state college system, and provides a process for individual course challenges.

## HOW STUDENTS LEARN ABOUT ASSESSMENT OF PRIOR LEARNING IN VERMONT

Various brochures and handouts are available to students at the sites of the state colleges. Advisors are generally aware of the program and refer students to either a brochure, directly to the OEP for more information, or to the Community College of Vermont website (*www.ccv.edu/apl*), which contains more information and gives times and dates of information sessions. Individual college advisors meet with prospective students and the staff also meets with interested students. Ninety-minute information sessions of are held in various locations around the state (usually at the Community College of Vermont sites, statewide, but also at educational fairs, or at specially requested meetings by large employers or agencies) and twice a year over the statewide Interactive Television Network. Any person interested in the process can attend one of these free sessions. At these sessions, the three steps in our process are described and explained:

1. Enrollment in the APL class and preparation of a portfolio.

2. Assessment of the portfolio by the Office of External Programs, a side arm of the Vermont State Colleges.

3. Issuance of a transcript that can used for transfer of credits to one of the Vermont State Colleges or a school of the student's choice that accepts experiential credits.

## ENROLLMENT IN THE PORTFOLIO ASSESSMENT PROGRAM

Any adult student may register for the portfolio preparation process. Prospective students learn about this option from their advisors, through newspaper stories, through advertised information sessions given around the state (in person with the program coordinator or via the statewide Interactive Television Network), through brochures distributed throughout the state, through word of mouth, and through websites. Enrollees in the process do not need to be degree students to enroll, can ask for credit in any curricular areas for which they feel qualified, and have no limit regarding the amount of credit they can request. The only prerequisites for enrolling in the course are (1) demonstrated college level writing skills through either transfer credit or satisfactory results on an assessment of writing, and (2) a requirement to meet with an advisor before enrolling to discuss if this is an appropriate option for the student. No minimum GPA is required. Often, the "Assessment of Prior Learning" course is one of the first courses an adult student will take, or is the first course after a long absence from college. All students are eligible; generally, they are not part of a "department" or have a degree plan as yet. There is no age limitation, although traditional-aged students very rarely are advised into the course since they usually will not yet possess college-level learning based on professional or community experience. There are, of course, always exceptions. (See Item 3, *Vermont State Colleges, A Student Handbook,* on the CD-ROM.)

## ASSESSMENT PRACTICES

### QUALIFICATIONS OF EVALUATORS

Portfolio evaluators are either full- or part-time faculty from colleges around the state, both specialists as well as "generalists" with broad knowledge about college curricula. At times, appropriate and qualified practitioners/experts are approved for this important task. Evaluators are generally required to have graduate or post-graduate degrees (See Item 2, *Vermont State Colleges, Evaluator Guidelines,* on the CD-ROM).

### STUDENTS' ORIENTATION TO DEVELOPING PORTFOLIOS

Students enroll in a three-credit college course that meets for a total of forty-two hours, usually once a week, for a fifteen-week semester. The course is taught by either part- or full-time faculty, depending on the institution offering the course. The course is offered at the Community College of Vermont mainly by part-time faculty hired specifically to teach this course, although some of these part-time faculty also teach other courses. Students must complete a portfolio to pass the course. While the portfolio itself does not receive a grade, students may receive a grade or choose a pass/fail option for this course.

Tuition and regular college fees, such as enrollment fees as required by the Vermont institution offering the course, are paid by students taking the course.

## THE PORTFOLIO SAMPLE: "PATSY SMITH"

The Vermont State Colleges portfolio document allows students to request as many credits as their experiential learning and advisors will allow. In the case of "Patsy Smith," Vermont State Colleges has submitted a "typical" rather than an exemplary portfolio, one in which format, layout, and individual parts are correct but in which there are weaknesses in documentation and titles of areas of study. The process is not necessarily designed for submission of one course-match portfolio; in this case, "Ms. Smith" is requesting consideration for twenty-one courses (sixty-three credits). The process forms, student essay, in addition to other items, are included on the CD-ROM. Examples are as follows:

◆ Patsy Committee Worksheet

◆ Patsy Cover Sheet

◆ Patsy Table of Contents

◆ Area of Study Request: Office Procedures (#1)

◆ Area of Study Request: Introduction to Special Education (#22)

◆ Patsy's Experiential Learning Essay

◆ Patsy's Resume

◆ Index to Documentation

◆ Letter of Documentation—Lehman

- ◆ Letter of Documentation—Terrell
- ◆ Letter of Documentation—Miller
- ◆ Letter of Documentation—Sellers
- ◆ Letter of Documentation—Folk music
- ◆ Letter of Documentation—Literature
- ◆ Bibliography

(See Item 1, *Portfolio Sample,* on the CD–ROM.)

## TRANSCRIPTING THE PORTFOLIO

Based on the result of the portfolio review, students receive a transcript from the Office of External Programs listing course equivalent titles and numbers of credits awarded.

## STEPS THROUGH THE VSC PORTFOLIO PROCESS

1. Students learn about assessment via word of mouth, newspaper article, or information-meeting announcement, Community College of Vermont website or advisor, other Vermont State Colleges staff or publications.

2. Student meets with an advisor at any of the colleges or Community Colleges of Vermont sites or with assessment staff to discuss the process and the student's placement in the course. Usually, the student must take a writing and reading assessment before enrolling in the course; writing skills must be at the level of a first-year college level English course.

3. The student enrolls in the three-credit course, Assessment of Prior Learning, and attends the class for one semester, learning to prepare a portfolio that articulates and documents the experiential learning.

4. At the end of the semester, the student submits portfolios to the Office of External Programs at the Vermont State Colleges.

5. The Coordinator of Assessment Services at the Office of External Programs reads and carefully reviews all portfolios, sorts the portfolios into groups of six to eight portfolios with similar content/curricular area requests, and hires four faculty members from colleges around the state to each review and evaluate the portfolios.

6. The group of reviewers convenes at the Office of External Programs for an "Advanced Standing Committee," chaired by the Assessment Coordinator.

7. After completion of this review meeting, a transcript of transfer credit is prepared for the student.

8. The student receives the transcript and transfers the awarded credits to a school/degree program of their choice that accepts experiential learning credits.

## FEES ASSOCIATED WITH PORTFOLIO ASSESSMENT

When enrolling in the "Assessment of Prior Learning" (APL) course, students pay the tuition required by the college offering the course, as well as a one-time assessment fee of $200. Also, students pay a $20 fee for the *APL Handbook.* Fees are not based on the amount of credit awarded. The "Assessment Fee" is a one-time fee, and used to pay an honorarium to the reviewing faculty.

## ASSESSOR COMPENSATION

An evaluator receives a $200 stipend for reading six to eight portfolios, and subsequently attending a day-long meeting with three other faculty to arrive at credit awards. Their mileage to the meeting is paid and they are served meals.

## USES OF TECHNOLOGY IN PORTFOLIO ASSESSMENT

Some APL courses are currently taught as "hybrid" courses; the class meets for eight to ten sessions face to face, and the rest of the class is held online. These students use Blackboard and an e-portfolio, but must still hand in a printed portfolio at the end of the class. Some faculty partially use Blackboard to supplement discussion and for individual contact with students regarding homework on parts of the portfolio.

## VERMONT STATE COLLEGES STATISTICAL PROFILE: 2006–2007

a. Total number of credits reviewed by portfolio assessment in the last academic year (Fall through Summer sessions of the academic year) 2006–2007:
   ◆ Credits reviewed/requested: 6,407
   ◆ Range of requests: 6 to 217

b. Average number of credits awarded based upon all students receiving "portfolio-awarded" credits during the academic year 2006–2007:
   ◆ Credits awarded: 4,670
   ◆ Range of awards: 5 to 99

c. Total number of students at the institution during the academic year 2006–2007: 146

d. Total number of students at the institution who participated in the Portfolio Assessment Program during the academic year 2006–2007: 146

**CD-ROM**

### *CD-ROM VERMONT STATE COLLEGES: ITEMS 1 TO 4*

1. Portfolio Sample: "Patsy Smith"

2. Evaluator Guidelines for Assessing Portfolios . . .

3. A Student Handbook for Educational Assessment and Portfolio Preparation

4. Assessment Outcomes

# THE UNIVERSITY OF ALABAMA
## EXTERNAL Degree Program

## Tuscaloosa, Alabama

Founded in 1831, The University of Alabama (enrollment 23,878; undergraduate 19,484) has been selected repeatedly as one of the top fifty public universities in the country (*Peterson's planner,* 2008). In addition to its academic reputation, the university is well known for its athletic teams and its services to adult learners. These aspects of the university converged recently with the university's Office of Public Relations' release of following announcement:

> Legendary Crimson Tide and NFL football star Joe Namath will receive his long-awaited college degree Saturday, Dec. 15, during The University of Alabama's winter commencement ceremonies . . .
>
> Over the past five years, Namath has worked to complete the requirement for his bachelor's degree through University of Alabama's External Degree program, known as EXD.
>
> EXD, an interdisciplinary program that allows adults to complete requirements for a bachelor's degree from University of Alabama, is the distance version of New College, a division of the College of Arts and Sciences. More than 1,500 students have graduated through this program, which was founded in 1973. (*University of Alabama News,* 2007, December 11).

## MISSION AND PURPOSE OF THE EXTERNAL DEGREE PROGRAM

The External Degree (EXD) Program, according to its website, "is an interdisciplinary undergraduate program through which adults complete requirements towards a Bachelor of Arts or Bachelor of Science degree (away from campus). An interdisciplinary degree is one that allows students to blend several areas of educational interests into meaningful curriculums to suit individual needs" (http://exd.ua.edu/). The EXD also offers adult students an opportunity to petition for an assessment of prior learning as one of several degree completion options available. In view of the EXD Program's mission of serving adult learners with significant professional experience, the academic recognition of prior learning is a fundamental component in the educational plan of many of its students. The concept is based on accepted principles of adult learning, which emphasize a participative, self-directed, problem-solving orientation to learning. It is designed to assist professional adult learners attain their academic and career goals by validating the professional competence they have acquired outside the classroom.

The integral place of prior learning assessment within the mission and purpose of the External Degree Program lies in its compatibility with the needs of the working adult student population served by the University. Based on the proven assumption that adults will bring a variety of diverse and often specialized skills to the classroom, experiential learning tends to emphasize the application of this knowledge; it challenges students to apply their theoretical and practical skills to the problems and needs of their community and workplace. By its very nature, experiential learning validates the richness and diversity of environments in which individuals can pursue meaningful learning.

## AN OVERVIEW OF PRIOR LEARNING ASSESSMENT

The standards and criteria developed by the EXD Program at The University of Alabama for assessing prior learning have remained virtually unchanged since the establishment of the EXD in the early 1970s. Through the years, this program has achieved a position of distinction in its field, and has served as a model for new and older universities that have chosen to add the assessment of prior learning to their programs. The EXD Program has worked closely with the American Council on Education (ACE) and the Council for Adult and Experiential Learning (CAEL). As a division of the university, EXD is also accredited by the Southern Association of Colleges and Schools (SACS) and adheres to its prescribed guidelines.

Academic credit may be awarded for college-level learning gained through life experiences. However, credit is not awarded for the student's merely having had the experiences; it is based on the ability to reflect on and articulate to faculty evaluators the college-level learning from those experiences. Experiences that may be the source of college-level learning include employment, volunteer activities, hobbies, private study, and in-service training.

## RATIONALE FOR PRIOR LEARNING ASSESSMENT

Most classroom learning begins with theories or ideas, not applications; that is, it is deductive learning moving from the general to the particular. This approach to learning is generally formal. It involves set periods of time, various exercises (such as writing papers), and periodic examinations.

Learning from experience is generally informal. It occurs in the midst of work, family, or recreational situations that rarely have set time periods, structured exercises, or periodic exams. Learning from experience usually consist of hands-on activities. It tends to be inductive; that is, it begins with particulars from which general principles can be derived.

Distinctions between classroom learning and learning from experience are not always consistent. Classroom learning may involve laboratories or other forms of testing ideas in practice. Learning from experience may also include laboratories, or be accompanied by reading and other forms of study, such as personal choice, hobby or employer direction. The chief difference is that classroom learning is structured so that credit hours can be awarded, usually with grades, based on the number of hours required to cover known measures of content. Learning from experience is organized differently. Students must extract from their experiences the guiding principles used in the academic fields that best relate to the experiences involved. These guiding principles must be illustrated and articulated to those who teach in the particular fields. This presentation, or portfolio, provides faculty with a basis for fairly assessing learning from experiences. Assessment can then be equated in credit units (semester hours) to what would have been earned in a similar classroom course.

Educational inputs (seat time in a traditional class, hours on the job, life experiences, etc.) do not guarantee learning outcomes, and if credit for learning is to be granted, it is essential that the evaluator have something upon which to base an evaluation. Classroom instructors use exams, papers, class participation, etc., as indicators that learning has taken place. The evaluator of experiential learning may use the portfolio—a formal written, oral, or electronic communication—to assess learning.

# THE PRIOR LEARNING PORTFOLIO

A prior learning portfolio is a document in which learning from various life experiences is organized into a manageable form for academic assessment. It is a way for the student to express what is known in a clear and concise manner, and permits accurate and efficient faculty assessment. In the portfolio the following questions should be answered:

◆ What are the life experiences and what is the learning?

◆ Is the learning equivalent to college-level learning?

◆ How can the college-level learning be documented?

Many adults have had a variety of experiences from which they have acquired college-level knowledge and skills. Business people often know sales techniques, business law, human resource management, bookkeeping, supervision, inventory control and/or marketing. Secretaries often know keyboarding, computer skills, business English, and office procedures. People who have written a great deal often know English composition and technical writing. A good many managers might know consumer economics and many people have public speaking abilities. Work with volunteer and human service organizations could lead to credit for management and counseling. If the knowledge and skills are at a college level, it is possible that college credit could be awarded through portfolio evaluation.

## TIMETABLE FOR PREPARING A PORTFOLIO

Once an "Application to Submit Knowledge" of Prior Learning (hereafter called an ASK) has been filed with and approved by the External Degree Prior Learning Coordinator, the student will have six months from the date of the letter of approval ("Go Letter") in which to prepare and submit the portfolio. If the student fails to submit the portfolio in that six-month period, the student will forfeit the evaluation fee and will have to resubmit an ASK to begin the process again should credit still be sought. (For the ASK document, see The University of Alabama, CD-ROM *Prior Learning Student Guide,* p. 18.)

## ASSISTANCE IN PREPARING A PORTFOLIO

A manual is provided to students wishing to apply for prior learning credit. Colvin's (2006) text on experiential learning is also recommended. Further, the Prior Learning Coordinator will provide guidance and bibliographic information on other texts about portfolio development. In addition, the student's academic adviser or the Prior Learning Coordinator can provide critiques of the drafts of the various portfolio elements. However, neither the adviser nor the Prior Learning Coordinator will serve as the portfolio assessor.

## TIME-LIMITS FOR ASSESSMENT OF A PORTFOLIO

The amount of time needed to complete the portfolio assessment varies, but it should be completed within six weeks after it has been submitted to the faculty assessor. The length of time may increase if the portfolio is submitted just prior to scheduled campus vacations such as Christmas or spring break. Every effort is made to get a timely evaluation.

## CREDIT LIMITATIONS FOR PRIOR LEARNING ASSESSMENT

If the student has invested time and care in the portfolio preparation, it should elicit credit. Because experience itself is not creditable, there is no way of knowing exactly how much credit a portfolio will render. The evaluator will recommend the number of credit hours to be awarded, and that recommendation will be weighed against any credit duplication, professional hours earned, and prior learning credit limits. Prior learning credit can be placed in any of the core requirement areas, in the depth study, or as elective credit. Portfolio credit may not be applied to the Senior Project. There is a limit of thirty hours (one-fourth of degree) of prior learning *portfolio* credit that any one student can earn. There is also a forty-five hour cumulative credit limit for all types of prior learning credit, which includes ACE credit, CLEP, Excelsior Exams, AP credit, DSST Exams (DANTES), and portfolio evaluation.

## PARTS OF A PORTFOLIO: ORGANIZATION FOR A "REGULAR ASK"

Each portfolio is creatively different, but each must contain the following elements. (Consult The University of Alabama CD-ROM, Item 2, *Prior Learning Student Guide,* beginning with p. 15.)

1. **Cover letter or transmittal letter**

2. **Title sheet (ASK)**

3. **Table of contents**

4. **Résumé**

5. **Detailed autobiographical description of experience and education**

   a. An introduction of the student, including education and career goals
   b. A description of how educational goals relate to family, work, and community life
   c. A description of the motivations for earning the undergraduate degree
   d. A conclusion that sums up the student's intention for earning credit through the assessment of prior learning

6. **Discussion of how this area of prior learning relates to the degree plan.** As directed on p. 15 of the *Prior Learning Student Guide* (hereafter referred to as the *Guide*): "The student should be as specific as possible about that part of the degree and/or the course requirement the prior learning credit will fulfill. Experiential learning will rarely parallel specific courses exactly; however, the student should identify the types of on-campus courses that sound similar to the student's past experiences." A detailed example of this process is also provided in a sample portfolio excerpt in the *Guide,* pp. 15–16.

7. **Detailed analysis of what the student has learned from the experience.** This is the section of the portfolio that some institutions and evaluators term the "analysis of learning" or the "life-learning" essay (*Guide,* p. 16). In the narrative the following questions should be answered:

   a. What was the subject matter or content learned from the experience?
   b. How did the student apply what was learned to the job or personal life?
   c. How can this knowledge be applied to other areas of life or to other jobs?
   d. What difference does it make in the student's life to have this knowledge?

e. Can the theories, rules, laws, guidelines or principles that have been earned from the experience be identified? [That is, can the credit received through the assessment of prior learning directly relate to the complexity of knowledge, regardless of how a particular subject was learned (McKenzie, 1992)?]

8. **Annotated Bibliography**

9. **Documentation**

## TRANSCRIPTING THE PORTFOLIO

Prior learning credit is listed on The University of Alabama transcript using course equivalent titles where applicable. Portfolio credit is usually recorded on the official transcript with a grade of P (or Pass). In a classroom course a faculty member has established specific criteria for the awarding of grades A, B, C or D; however, such criteria are not usually available for a portfolio and the learning rarely exactly duplicates a course.

## TRANSFERABILITY OF PRIOR LEARNING CREDITS

If an External Degree student wishes to use The University of Alabama prior learning credit in degree programs at other universities or colleges, there is no assurance or guarantee that these credits will be transferable. Students should ask this question of colleges or universities they wish to attend.

Likewise, The University of Alabama External Degree Program will make transfer determinations on a case-by-case basis for acceptance of transcribed prior learning credit awarded by other regionally accredited colleges and universities.

## FEES ASSOCIATED WITH PRIOR LEARNING ASSESSMENT

There is an evaluation fee of $500.00 that must be paid on-line after the ASK form has been approved. If the student is submitting a "Modified ASK" (CD-ROM, the *Guide*, p. 20) for standardized American Council on Education (ACE) credit, a fee of $150.00 will be charged. These fees are for the evaluation and are subject to change.

## APPEALING THE CREDIT DECISION OF THE EVALUATOR

A carefully prepared portfolio generally earns academic credit. However, sometimes students have unrealistic goals and are disappointed if they do not receive as much credit as they had hoped. The evaluation may show that the student needs to learn additional concepts or take additional courses in order to develop more fully the competencies in any field of study. If the student is dissatisfied with the evaluation, a request for another evaluation may be filed in the form of a letter petitioning a second evaluation. If the request is granted, an additional evaluation fee of $150.00 will be charged.

## CURRENCY OF KNOWLEDGE

Currency is important in many academic areas. If experiences are old, it is unlikely that the student's knowledge of theories in that field is current.

## PORTFOLIO PROCESS

Campus courses are updated on a regular basis.
The External Degree Program has specific procedures for submitting evidence of prior learning. All portfolio submissions must be preceded by the submission of a *Regular ASK* (See CD-ROM, Item 2, *Guide,* p. 18). The following is a step-by-step explanation of this process for the student.

1. Discuss the submission of an *ASK* (See CD-ROM, Item 2, *Guide,* p. 18) or *Modified ASK* (*Guide,* p. 20) with the adviser.

    a. Complete the Pre-*ASK* checklist.
    b. Complete the *ASK* and return it with all attachments to the External Degree offices. Once the *ASK* is processed, the student will be notified to make the evaluation payment online at *MyBama.ua.edu.*

2. Once the *ASK* is received by External Degree offices the procedure is as follows:

    a. The student makes payment of the evaluation fee.
    b. The *ASK* and attachments are examined by the Prior Learning Coordinator. The *ASK* may be returned for clarification, correction, or additional information.
    c. If the *ASK* is in order, it is "staffed" (introduced at the weekly staff meeting where its viability is determined).
    d. If the *ASK* is viable, the student is sent a *"GO"* email stating that the student may begin the process of portfolio preparation. The student is given six months to prepare the portfolio.

3. The student will receive a fifth-month email as a reminder that there is one month left to prepare the portfolio.

4. If the student fails to submit the portfolio within the six-month period, the evaluation fee is forfeited. If the student wishes to submit the portfolio after the six months, another *ASK* and fee is required.

5. When the portfolio arrives in the External Degree office, it is logged in by the Prior Learning Coordinator.

    a. A permission form is sent to the head of the evaluator's department for approval of service.

    b. Once the permission form is approved and returned, the evaluator is contacted and the portfolio is delivered to the evaluator.

    c. The evaluator may take up to four weeks to evaluate and return the portfolio. During that time the evaluator may contact the Prior Learning Coordinator, the student's adviser, colleagues, or the student.

6. When the portfolio is returned with the evaluation, it is logged by the Registrar, who will check for duplication, credit title, and credit amounts. The evaluation form must then be signed by the student's adviser and the External Degree Director. The Registrar will notify the University Records office of awarded credit.

7. The student will then be notified about the awarding of credit.

8. The portfolio will be retained in the External Degree offices as a record of the credit attempt until the student graduates.

## MODIFIED PORTFOLIOS

Occasionally students pursue credit for learning experiences that have been evaluated and assigned credit recommendations by national groups such as the American Council on Education. Because pre-existing (pre-determined) credits are pursued in a slightly different manner, the process for compiling and submitting the portfolio is "modified."

"Modified" portfolios are used only when students wish to claim credits that have pre-determined recommendations; for example, military training, Dale Carnegie courses, AT&T courses and/or for specific examinations such as Novell. Because credit awarded depends on the breadth and depth of the learning and the currency and applicability of the knowledge to the student's degree plan, credit hours awarded for each certification, license, or school may vary.

Prior learning credits are viewed as more than just a way to accumulate credit. To ensure that students best demonstrate and maximize the learning for fullest possible credit recommendation, submissions for modified portfolio presentations should, therefore, be handled in the following manner:

### MODIFIED ASK

1. Title page that indicates the subject matter and a brief statement of where any credit earned should be applied.

2. A brief chronological description of learning experience. This is important because ACE recommendations are dated and credit recommendations may depend on the date of participation. It is also important when using licenses to check for currency.

3. Description of the learning experience (no more than two to three pages in length). This helps fill in gaps for needed information that may not always be apparent on certifications.

4. Analysis of the learning experience (no more than two to three pages in length). This must include discussion on the currency of the knowledge and explain how the learning applies to the degree plan. Mere exposure to the learning does not warrant college credit; the analysis should include a summary of what was learned and how it fits into the degree plan.

5. Documentation of the learning experience (certificates, licenses, official school transcripts, DD214 or DD295, SMART or ARRTS transcripts, etc.).

NOTE: The student should always discuss the submission of the Modified Portfolio with his or her adviser and the Prior Learning Coordinator before actual submission to the External Degree Program. The student will be notified to submit the evaluation fee online before finalization of the evaluation.

## THE UNIVERSITY OF ALABAMA, EXTERNAL DEGREE PROGRAM STATISTICAL PROFILE: 2006–2007

a. Total number of credits reviewed by portfolio assessment in the last academic year (Fall through Summer sessions of the academic year) 2006–2007: 45

b. Average number of credits awarded based upon all students receiving "portfolio-awarded" credits during the academic year 2006–2007: 12

c. Total number of students at the institution during the academic year 2006–2007: 500 in the External Degree program

d. Total number of students at the institution who participated in the Portfolio Assessment Program during the academic year 2006–2007: 4

### CD-ROM, THE UNIVERSITY OF ALABAMA: ITEMS 1 TO 3

CD-ROM

1. Portfolio Sample: Management

2. Prior Learning Student Guide

3. Assessment Outcomes

# CONTRIBUTORS AND AFFILIATIONS

## Ashford University

400 N. Bluff Boulevard, Clinton, Iowa 52732
http://www.ashford.edu
*Primary Contributor:* Karen Conzett

## Athabasca University

1 University Drive, Athabasca, Alberta, Canada T9S 3A3
http://www.athabascau.ca
*Primary Contributor:* Dianne Conrad

## Charter Oak State College

55 Paul J. Manafort Drive, New Britain, Connecticut 06053
www.charteroak.edu
*Primary Contributor:* Maryanne R. LeGrow

## Council for Adult and Experiential Learning

55 East Monroe Street, Suite 1930, Chicago, IL 60602
http://www.cael.org/
*Primary Contributors:* Diana Bamford-Rees and Judith B. Wertheim

## Depaul University

School for New Learning
25 East Jackson Boulevard, Chicago, Illinois 60604
http://www.depaul.edu/
*Primary Contributors:* Morry Fiddler and Catherine Marineau

## Empire State College

One Union Avenue, Saratoga Springs, New York 12866
http://www.esc.edu/
*Primary Contributor:* Nan L. Travers
*Additional Contributors:* Alan Mandell, Marnie Evans, and Paul Alberti

## Regis University

3333 Regis Boulevard, L-4, Denver, Colorado 80221
http://www.regis.edu/
*Primary Contributor:* Fran Kehoe

## St. Edward's University

3001 S. Congress Avenue, C/M 1040, Austin, Texas 78704
http://www.stedwards.edu
*Primary Contributor:* Susan C. Gunn

## St. Joseph's College

245 Clinton Avenue, Brooklyn, New York 11205
http://www.sjcny.edu/
*Primary Contributor:* Linda F. Fonte
*Additional Contributor:* Debra MacDonald

## Sinclair Community College

444 W. Third Street, Dayton, Ohio 45402
http://sinclair.edu/
*Primary Contributor:* Carolyn Mann

## Spring Arbor University

106 E. Main Street, Spring Arbor, Michigan 49283
http://www.arbor.edu/
*Primary Contributor:* Jan Hultman
*Additional Contributor:* Natalie Gianetti

## The University of Alabama

External Degree Program
College of Continuing Studies, Box 870388
307 Martha Parham Hall-West, Tuscaloosa, Alabama 35487
http://exp.ua.edu/
*Primary Contributor:* Kevin J. Thornthwaite

## Valdosta State University

1500 North Patterson Street, Valdosta, Georgia 31698
http://www.valdosta.edu/
*Primary Contributor:* Gerald A. (Jerry) Merwin, Jr.
*Additional Contributors:* Sharon L. Gravett, Barbara Stanley, Mary Ellen
    Dallman, Heather Brasell, Christine James, Sean Lennon, Jim Nienow,
    Beverley Blake, Karen Shepard, Arsalan Wares, Cheri Tillman, and
    Gayle Taylor

## Vermont State Colleges

Office of External Programs
32 College Street, Schulmaier Hall, Suite 201
Montpelier, Vermont 05602
http://www.ccv.edu
*Primary Contributor:* Gabrielle Dietzel

# TERMS AND ABBREVIATIONS ASSOCIATED WITH PRIOR LEARNING ASSESSMENT

**AACRAO**

The American Association of Collegiate Registrars and Admissions Officers

**Abbreviations for Prior Learning Assessment**

| | |
|---|---|
| **APCL** | Assessment of Prior Certificated Learning (U.K.) |
| **APEL** | Assessment of Prior Experiential Learning (Ireland, U.K., U.S.) |
| **APL** | Assessment of Prior Learning (U.K.) |
| **EVC** | Erkennen Vanelders of Informed Verworven Competencies (Netherlands) |
| **PLA** | Prior Learning Assessment (U.S., Canada) |
| **PLAR** | Prior Learning Assessment and Recognition (Canada) |
| **RDA** | Reconnaissance des Acquis (Canada) |
| **RPL** | Recognition of Prior Learning (Australia, South Africa, New Zealand) |

**ACE**

American Council on Education (*www.acenet.edu*). ACE has reviewed thousands of training programs from corporations, labor unions, government agencies, schools, and the military for college credit recommendations.

**ACT**

American College Testing program. Administrators of aptitude and achievement tests.

**AP Examinations**

A national testing program, administered by The College Board, that provides thirty-seven courses and exams across twenty-two subject areas.

**APCL**

Assessment of Prior Certificated Learning (U.K.)

**APEL**

Assessment of Prior Experiential Learning (Ireland, U.K., U.S.)

**APL**

Assessment of Prior Learning (U.K.)

**Articulation**

An agreement or set of agreements among institutions or programs that compare courses and specify equivalencies; the agreements are most often based on intended outcomes, coverage of subject matter, or credits.

On an individual basis, the relationship of a person's learning being assessed for credit to academic, personal, or professional goals.

**Assessment**

A term that includes a full range of procedures and strategies to gain information about a student's knowledge; also referred to as Evaluation.

**Assessment Evidence**

(*see also* Evidence of Learning).

A product, artifact, or means by which an individual demonstrates her/his learning or capabilities that is amenable to public review and assessment (e.g., portfolio, demonstration, exam, simulation, or presentation).

**Assessor**

An individual with appropriate knowledge and skill who is responsible for measuring a person's learning.

**Block Credit Model**

The assignment of a variable number of credits to an individual's assessed evidence of learning based on a judgment of its breadth and depth as well as its relationship to the existing curriculum of the institution.

**CAEL**

The Council for Adult and Experiential Learning, a national non-profit organization that creates and manages effective learning strategies for working adults through partnerships with employers, higher education, government and labor. CAEL publishes the standards for the assessment of learning that colleges use to create policies and procedures for their program. CAEL is the publisher of this text (*www.cael.org*).

**Certificate**

An artifact or document verifying participation in training or another organized learning experience. Certificates may represent levels of that participation, ranging from only attendance to attendance with assessment of the desired learning outcomes.

**Challenge Exam**

A test of an individual's learning that is based on the expected outcomes of a course (or set of courses) in an institution's curriculum.

**CHEA**

The Council on Higher Education Accreditation, an organization of six regional accrediting bodies.

**CLEP**

The College-Level Examination Program is a national program that provides examinations in a number of subject matters allowing students to earn college credit for their learning (*www.collegeboard.com*).

**College-Level Learning**

A standard set by a post-secondary institution to define the level of learning worthy of credit. Academia has used several definitions of college-level learning (e.g., a mix of theory and application or ideas and their application; the integration and interpretation of one's experiences using accepted ideas or theories; complexity of cognitive, perceptual, and behavioral dimensions of learning).

In response to the multiple sources and circumstances in which creditable learning can occur, several options have been used for determining college level in the assessment of prior learning; for example: relating the content of learning to subject areas traditionally taught in colleges; showing that what was learned is at a level of achievement equal to what is commonly recognized by (other) colleges; comparing specific learning to that acquired in college-level curricula; relating learning to a personal goal that requires college-level learning; and identifying learning as that acquired after high school and expected for professional acceptance.

**COLLO**

The Coalition of Lifelong Learning Organizations (COLLO), formally established in 1973, consists of national associations and groups that share a common interest in enhancing the field of lifelong learning, i.e., adult and continuing education, throughout the nation. These organizations represent public schools, institutions of higher education, industry, labor groups, and most importantly, the learners themselves (*http://www.thecollo.org/aboutus.php#purposes*).

**Competence**

A demonstrable capability based on specific knowledge within a certain context.

**Competence-Based Credit Model**

The assignment of credit to demonstrated and assessed competence rather than to a specific body of knowledge or subject matter.

**Course Challenge**

A request for credit based on the demonstration of knowledge, specified learning outcomes, or competence equivalent to an existing course in a curriculum.

**Course Equivalence Credit Model**

The assignment of credit only for the demonstration of knowledge or learning equivalent to an existing course with a specified number of associated credits in a curriculum.

### Credit

A credit is typically one hour of instruction per week for a term of one semester (about sixteen weeks) or a quarter (about twelve weeks). Most colleges in the United States judge students' progress toward a degree by their accumulation of credit hours. A typical course meets three hours per week; such a course successfully completed by a student results in three hours of credit. If the institution operates on a semester schedule, the student earns three semester hours of credit; if on a quarter system, the student earns three quarter hours of credit (two-thirds of the semester credit).

### Credit Bank

An agency that allows individuals to bank evidence of academic or professional achievement; this allows an individual to accumulate credit from a variety of sources over an extended period of time in a single repository. The Open Learning Agency in Canada offers this service, for example.

### Criteria

An articulated set of specifications by which someone's learning (or evidence of learning) may be measured and evaluated. Assessment criteria often cover variables such as authenticity, sufficiency, and currency of learning; the effectiveness of a criterion is measured by both its validity and reliability. (Is it useful in measuring what it intends to measure? Would subsequent assessments of the same evidence produce similar results?)

### DANTES

The Defense Activity for Non-Traditional Education Support regulates financial aid programs for active military and administers equivalency exams for military and civilians (see *www.getcollegecredit.com/*).

### Distance Education

Also called *distributed education* or *distance learning.*

The engagement in an educational activity when the learner is studying at a distance from the source of instruction; frequently, and in contrast to face-to-face situations, the distance between learner and instructor is accompanied by asynchronicity (i.e., communications are separated by time as well as physical space). Increasingly, this form of education is mediated and aided by various forms of both communication and storage technology.

### DSST (DANTES Subject Standard Tests)

Equivalency exams for military and civilians (see *http://www.getcollege credit.com*)

### Evidence of Learning

(*see also* Assessment Evidence)
Documents, artifacts, or other products that represent what a person knows or can do (i.e., has learned) and that are used to substantiate an individual's claim for credit in an assessment process. Evidence may be direct (what the person says or represents regarding his/her learning) or indirect (what others say about the learning).

## Evaluation

The determination of the quality of an individual's learning relative to standards.

## EVC

Erkennen Vanelders of Informed Verworven Competencies (Netherlands)

## Experiential Learning

Learning that has been gained as a result of reflecting upon the events or experiences in one's life in contrast to formal education.

## Feedback

Commentary offered to an individual that addresses the quality of the evidence submitted for assessment. Some of the qualities of feedback are clarity, integrity (with respect to public criteria), flexibility (in the recognition of various expressions of learning), empathy (in the communication style), and timeliness.

## Goal(s) Statement

One of the components of a portfolio or other evidence presented for assessment for credit. The intent of a goals statement is to help an individual in the PLA process clarify her/his short- and long-term personal, professional, or educational goals to set a context for the assessment process.

## Learning from Experience

A process by which an individual may determine what he/she has identified as meaningful and potentially creditable from the events and experiences of his/her life.

## Learning Outcome

A statement of measurable (or anticipated) learning that describes what a person should know and/or be able to do as a result of a (formal or informal) learning experience.

## Letter of Testimony

A letter or document prepared by someone who is appropriately qualified to substantiate a person's claim of knowledge or skills because of direct observation of that person. Letters of testimony often constitute some or all of the evidence of learning in an individual's request for credit in an assessment process.

## Lifelong Learning

As a noun, this is the learning gained in both formal and informal situations that a person accumulates over the course of her/his life. As a verb, it is the process(es) of gaining knowledge in formal and informal situations (i.e., the full range of life's experiences).

### Measurement of Learning

One of the steps in a prior learning assessment process that entails determining the degree and level of learning an individual has achieved.

### Mentoring

The process of helping another person develop skills, knowledge, attitudes, and/or values through various strategies, including modeling of these attributes, advising, coaching, and promoting other activities that contribute to advancing the person's capabilities and capacities. In an assessment process, mentoring may serve as an important bridge between identifying creditable learning and articulating the appropriate evidence for its assessment and measurement.

### Nonsponsored Learning

(Also called *nonformal learning*)
Organized events or unplanned results of life or work experiences; skills and knowledge gained through unstructured events and experiences.

### Open Learning

A philosophy of education that increases access to education so that anyone can study anything at any place and at any time is called open learning. An institution that supports open learning is usually characterized by open or flexible admissions policies, flexible start and completion dates, courses offered via a variety of media and methodologies, recognition of credentials from other institutions or sources, and recognition of the learning from experience and lifelong learning.

### Open Learning Agency

A publicly funded organization in British Columbia, Canada, that has a specialty in the delivery of distance education and training; the agency coordinates its activities with industries, government, and educational partners

### PLA

Prior Learning Assessment (U.S., Canada)

### PLAR

Prior Learning Assessment and Recognition (Canada)

### Portfolio

A collection of evidence in support of a person's claim for credit through a prior learning assessment process.

### Portfolio Development

The process of identifying and creating documentation or other evidence of learning to be organized for presentation in support of a claim(s) for credit via a prior learning assessment process. In some programs or institutions, the portfolio development is assisted by a course to structure a step-by-step process.

### Prerequisite

A requirement—often a course or program (or its equivalent)—that must be successfully completed by an assessment process before participating or enrolling in an advanced course or program.

### Principles of Assessment

The standards and guidelines that guide the processes, activities, and quality assurance of the processes for measuring and evaluating learning.

### Prior Learning Assessment (PLA)

A process by which an individual's learning from experience is assessed and evaluated for purposes of granting credit, certification, or advanced standing toward further education or training.

### Quality Assurance

Efforts and associated processes to ensure that standards are being met.

### RDA

Reconnaissance des Acquis (Canada)

### RPL

Recognition of Prior Learning (Australia, South Africa, New Zealand)

### Residency Requirement

A minimum number of credits an institution requires of students to be awarded a credential, such as a degree, from that institution.

### Self-assessment

An activity and process by which an individual describes and judges the nature, extent, and level of one's own learning or performance. Self-assessment is a component of reflection and it is often a part of, or an outcome of, a prior learning assessment process.

### Self-directed Learning

The type of learning in which an individual takes responsibility for identifying, goal setting, managing, and assessing or seeking assessment. Self-directed learning does not mean learning alone because one may choose the strategies for learning collaboratively or in structured situations as an option for directing his/her learning.

### Skill Set

A grouping of complementary skills that constitute a larger or more abstract role—for example, the skill set for a manager may include communications, performance evaluation, expertise of the industry, analytic and systemic thinking, and interpersonal abilities.

### Sponsored Learning

Pre-planned learning experiences offered by a postsecondary institution.

**Transcript**

The formal record of a student's achievement in an academic institution or certification program.

**Transfer Credit**

The recognition of credits earned in one institution by another institution.

**Transferable Skills**

Knowledge, capabilities, attitudes or values that are effective across multiple contexts, such as various workplaces or organizations.

# REFERENCES

## Introduction

Council for Adult and Experiential Learning. (2000). *Serving adult learners in adult education, principles of effectiveness: Executive summary.* Retrieved August 17, 2008, from http://www.cael.org/alfi/PDF%20files/Summary%20of%20Alfi%20Principles%20of%20Effectiveness.pdf

Council for Adult and Experiential Learning. (1999). *Serving adult learners in higher education, findings from CAEL's benchmarking study: Executive summary.* Chicago: Author.

Harms, B. K. (2008). *Serving adult students: What really matters? The "must do" list for colleges and universities.* Retrieved August 17, 2008, from http://www.stamats.com/resources/publications/whitepapers/pdfs/WhitePaper18.pdf

Sevier, R. A. (2008, February). *Major trends: Factors that will impact your ability to recruit students, raise dollars, and market your institution.* Presented at the 2008 National Association of Independent Colleges and Universities Conference, Washington, D.C.

Trent, B., & Chen, H. L. (2008). *Next generation e-portfolio.* Retrieved July 30, 2008, from https://www.academicimpressions.com/whitepaper/0808-e-wp.pdf

## Chapter 1

Council for Adult and Experiential Learning. (1999). *25th Anniversary: CAEL timeline 1974–1999.* Chicago: Author.

Council for Adult and Experiential Learning. (2007). *Prior learning assessment at home and abroad.* Chicago: Author.

Colvin, J. (2006). *Earn college credit for what you know* (4th ed.). Chicago, IL: CAEL.

Evans, N. (2000). *Experiential learning around the world: Employability and the global economy.* London: Jessica Kingsley Publishers.

Fiddler, M., Marienau, C., & Whitaker, U. (2006). *Assessing learning: Standards, principles, and procedures* (2nd ed.). Chicago, IL: CAEL.

Fugate, M., & Chapman, R. (1992). *Prior learning assessment: Results of a nationwide institutional survey.* Chicago, IL: CAEL.

Gamson, Z. (1989). *Higher education and the real world: The story of CAEL.* Wolfeboro, NH: Longwood Academic.

Lamdin, L. (1992). *Earn college credit for what you know* (3rd ed.). Chicago, IL: CAEL.

McIntyre, V. (1981). *Wherever you learned it: A directory of opportunities for educational credit.* Columbia, MD: CAEL.

Simosko, S. (1985). *Earn college credit for what you know.* Washington, D.C.: Acropolis Books, Ltd.

Whitaker, U. (1989). *Assessing learning: Standards, principles, and procedures.* Philadelphia, PA: CAEL.

Zucker, B., Johnson, C., & Flint, T. (1999). *Prior learning assessment: A guidebook to American institutional practices.* Chicago, IL: CAEL.

## Chapter 2

Council for Adult and Experiential Learning. (2008). *Adult learning in focus: National and state-by-state data.* Retrieved August 11, 2008, from http://www.cael.org/pdf/State_Indicators_Monograph.pdf

Council for Adult and Experiential Learning. (2008). *State policies to bring adult learning into focus: A companion guide.* Retrieved August 11, 2008, from http://www.cael.org/pdf/State_Indicators_Policy_Guide.pdf

Kentucky Council on Postsecondary Education. (2008). *Double the numbers: Kentucky's plan to increase college graduates.* Retrieved August 11, 2008, from http://cpe.ky.gov/doublethenumbers/

Kentucky Council on Postsecondary Education. (2008). *Adult learner initiative.* Retrieved August 11, 2008 from http://cpe.ky.gov/policies/academicinit/adult_learner.htm

Minnesota State Colleges and Universities Board of Trustees. (2008, May). *Proposed policy 3.35 credit for prior learning.* Retrieved August, 2008, from http://www.mnscu.edu/board/materials/2008/may21/asa-05-proposed_335.pdf

Oklahoma State Regents. (2006). *Reach higher: Oklahoma's degree completion program.* Retrieved August 11, 2008, from http://www.okhighered.org/reachinghigher/earn-credit.shtml

Oklahoma State Regents. (2006). *Reach higher: Oklahoma's degree completion program.* Retrieved August 11, 2008, from http://www.okhighered.org/student-center/college-stdnts/academic/extra-learning.shtml

Pennsylvania Workforce Development. (2006, August 6). *Governor Rendell combats critical workforce issues with credit-for-experience initiative.* Retrieved August, 2008, from http://www.paworkforce.state.pa.us/media/cwp/view.asp?a=470&q =156432

Pennsylvania Workforce Development. (2007, August 8). *Press releases.* Retrieved August, 2008, from http://www.paworkforce.state.pa.us/professionals/cwp/view.asp?a=11&q=157055

Pennsylvania Workforce Development. (2008, September 30). *Governor Rendell's strategy for building a skilled workforce.* Retrieved October, 2008, from http://www.paworkforce.state.pa.us/about/cwp/view.asp?a=471&q=152120

## Chapter 3

Fiddler, M., Marienau, C., & Whitaker, U. (2006). *Assessing learning: Standards, principles, and procedures.* Dubuque, IA: Kendall/Hunt.

## Chapter 4

Mann, C. (1998). *Credit for lifelong learning* (5th ed.). Bloomington, IN: Tichenor.

Whitaker, U. G. (1989). *Assessing learning: standards, principles, and procedures.* Philadelphia: Council for Adult & Experiential Learning.

Willingham, W. W. (1977). *Principles of good practice in assessing experiential learning.* Columbia, MD: Council for Adult & Experiential Learning.

## Chapter 5

Ashford University. (n.d.). *Accreditation.* Retrieved June 12, 2008, from http://www.ashford.edu/info/accreditation.php

Ashford University. (n.d.). *Casino operations artifact.* Clinton, IA: Author.

Ashford University. (n.d.). *EXP 200 experiential essay course description.* Clinton, IA: Author.

Ashford University. (n.d.). *Healing touch credit rationale paper.* Clinton, IA: Author.

Ashford University. (n.d.). *Healing touch documentation.* Clinton, IA: Author.

Ashford University. (n.d.). *Mission Statement.* Retrieved June 12, 2008, from http://www.ashford.edu/info/

Ashford University. (n.d.). *PLA documentation guide.* Retrieved June 12, 2008, from http://www.ashford.edu/online/forms/PLAGuide.pdf

Ashford University. (n.d.). *PLA flow charts.* Clinton, IA: Author.

Ashford University. (n.d.). *PLA quality assurance model.* Clinton, IA.: Author.

Ashford University. (n.d.). *Portfolio sample: Experiential essay, casino operations.* Clinton, IA: Author.

## Chapter 6

Athabasca University. (2008, June 13). *About Athabasca University.* Retrieved July 6, 2008, from http://www.athabascau.ca/aboutAU/

Athabasca University. (n.d.). *Assessors' response sheet.* Alberta, Canada: Author.

Athabasca University Centre for Learning Accreditation. (2008, May 27). *By portfolio.* Retrieved July 6, 2008, from http://priorlearning.athabascau.ca/by-portfolio.php

Athabasca University Centre for Learning Accreditation. (n.d.). *Course-based assessment form.* Alberta, Canada: Author.

Athabasca University. (n.d.). *Criteria table version for program: Bachelor of professional arts and human services.* Alberta, Canada: Author.

Athabasca University. (n.d.). *Guidelines for portfolio assessors.* Alberta, Canada: Author.

Athabasca University. (2008, June 6). *Mission & mandate.* Retrieved July 6, 2008, from http://www.athabascau.ca/aboutAU/mission.php

Athabasca University. (n.d.). *Portfolio sample: Bachelor of professional arts and human services, program-based portfolio.* Alberta, Canada: Author.

Athabasca University Centre for Learning Accreditation. (2008, May 27). *Prior learning assessment and recognition (PLAR).* Retrieved July 6, 2008, from http://priorlearning.athabascau.ca/index.php

Athabasca University's PLAR, Centre for Learning Accreditation. (n.d.). *Prior learning assessment and recognition.* Retrieved July 6, 2008, from http://priorlearning.athabascau.ca/documents/PLAR%20pamphlet.pdf

Athabasca University. (n.d.). *Prior learning assessment and recognition (PLAR) at Athabasca University: A handbook for preparing portfolios.* Alberta, Canada: Author.

Conrad, D. (2007, May 16). *Practicing PLAR at Athabasca University: Overviewing a complex system at the Alberta Council on Admissions and Transfer workshop. (PPT).* Retrieved July 8, 2008, from http://www.acat.gov.ab.ca/plar/ppt/DianneConrad_PracticingPLARatAthabascaUniversity.pps#256,1, Practicing PLAR at Athabasca University: Overviewing a Complex System. ACAT Workshop, May 16, 2007.

## CHAPTER 7

Charter Oak State College. (n.d.). *Faculty guidelines for portfolio assessment.* New Britain, CT: Author.

Charter Oak State College. (n.d.). *About us.* Retrieved July 15, 2008, from http://www.charteroak.edu/AboutUs/

Charter Oak State College. (n.d.). *Portfolio assessment.* Retrieved July 15, 2008, from http://www.charteroak.edu/Current/Programs/Portfolio/assessment.cfm

Charter Oak State College. (n.d.). *Frequently asked questions.* Retrieved July 15, 2008, from http://www.charteroak.edu/Current/Programs/ Portfolio/faq.cfm#q1

Charter Oak State College. (n.d.). *Portfolio process flow chart.* New Britain, CT: Author.

Charter Oak State College. (n.d.). *Portfolio sample: Pedagogical grammar.* New Britain, CT: Author.

Charter Oak State College. (n.d.). *Student handbook.* Retrieved July 15, 2008, from http://www.charteroak.edu/Current/Forms/StudentHandbook2007-2008.pdf

Charter Oak State College. *Syllabus: IDS 102 prior learning portfolio development.* New Britain, CT: Author.

## CHAPTER 8

Empire State College, State University of New York. (2004, November). *A student guide: Credit for prior college-level learning.* Saratoga Springs, NY: Author.

Empire State College, State University of New York. (n.d.). *About Empire State College.* Retrieved June 6, 2008, from http://www.esc.edu/esconline/online2.nsf/html/isescforyou.html

Empire State College, State University of New York. (n.d.). *Assessment resources.* Retrieved June 6, 2008, from http://www.esc.edu/esconline/across_esc/assessment.nsf/home.html

Empire State College, State University of New York. (n.d.). *Credit for prior learning.* Retrieved June 6, 2008, from http://www.esc.edu.esconline/across_esc/cdl/cdl.nsf/wholeshortlinks2/Credit+for+Prior+Learning

Empire State College, State University of New York. (n.d.). *Individual prior learning assessment policy and procedures. Evaluation process and credit recommendation.* Retrieved June 6, 2008, from http://www.esc.edu/ESConline/ESCdocuments/policies.nsf/allbysubject/Individual+Prior+Learning+Assessment+Policy+and+Procedures

Empire State College, State University of New York. (2008, February). *Fact sheet.* Saratoga Springs, NY: Author.

Empire State College, State University of New York. (n.d.). *Individual prior learning assessment policy and procedures. Limits on prior learning requests placed with one evaluator.* Retrieved June 6, 2008, from http://www.esc.edu/ESConline/ESCdocuments/policies.nsf/allbysubject/Individual+Prior+Learning+Assessment+Policy+and+Procedures

Empire State College, State University of New York. (n.d.). *Portfolio sample: Environmental advocacy, organizing and research excerpt.* Saratoga Springs, NY: Author.

Empire State College, State University of New York. (n.d.). *Prior learning evaluation (faculty evaluation) edited excerpt.* Saratoga Springs, NY: Author.

Empire State College, State University of New York. (2007, May). *Student degree planning guide, 2007–2008.* Saratoga Springs, NY: Author.

Empire State College, State University of New York. (2008, February). *Viewbook 2008.* Saratoga Springs, NY: Author.

# Chapter 9

Regis University. (n.d.). *Setting up an iWebfolio account.* Retrieved July 30, 2008, from http://academic.regis.edu/ed202/jobaids/stuacctsetup.htm

Regis University. (n.d.). *ED202: Prior learning assessment (portfolio) course information.* Retrieved July 30, 2008, from http://academic.regis.edu/ed202

Regis University. *Online orientation.* Retrieved July 30, 2008, from http://spsundergradorientation.org

Regis University. (n.d.). *Our mission.* Retrieved October 8, 2008, from http://www.regis.edu/regis.asp?sctn=abt

Regis University. (2007, Summer). *Prior learning assessment department policies and procedures.* Retrieved August 10, 2008, from http://academic.regis.edu/ed202/policies.htm#Specific%20Regis%20Academic%20Degree%20Requirements

Regis University. (n.d.). *Standards for awarding credit through portfolio assessment.* Retrieved August 8, 2008, from http://academic.regis.edu/ed202/policies.htm#STANDARDS%20FOR%20AWARDING%20CREDIT%20THROUGH%20PRIOR%20LEARNING%20ASSESSMENT

Regis University. (n.d.). *Learners becoming leaders in the Jesuit Catholic tradition.* Retrieved July 30, 2008, from www.regis.edu

# Chapter 10

Haslam, B. (n.d). *Who are Free Methodists?* Retrieved August 2, 2008, from http://www.freemethodistchurch.org/Sections/About%20Us/Basic%20Info/FAQs/What's%20A%20Free%20Methodist.htm

Hultman, J. (2008, Spring). *Writing a life-learning paper.* Spring Arbor, MI: Spring Arbor University.

Spring Arbor University. (2008). *About Spring Arbor University.* Retrieved August 2, 2008, from http://www.arbor.edu/about/index.aspx

Spring Arbor University. (n.d.). *Evaluator rubric.* Spring Arbor, MI: Author.

Spring Arbor University. (n.d.). *Evaluator training handbook.* Spring Arbor, MI: Author.

Spring Arbor University. (n.d.). *Life-learning experience paper guideline, health issues.* Spring Arbor, MI: Author.

Spring Arbor University. (n.d.). *Life-learning experience paper guideline, marriage and family.* Spring Arbor, MI: Author.

Spring Arbor University. (n.d.). *Life-learning experience paper guideline, psychology of adjustment.* Spring Arbor, MI: Author.

Spring Arbor University. (n.d.). *Portfolio sample: WRT 312 critical analysis and research writing.* Spring Arbor, MI: Author.

Spring Arbor University. (n.d.). *Professional schools and training handbook.* Spring Arbor, MI: Author.

Spring Arbor University. (n.d.). *PST handout for students, assessment information.* Spring Arbor, MI: Author.

Spring Arbor University. (n.d.). *Training on the Rubric for LLP Evaluators.* (PPT). Spring Arbor, MI: Author.

Spring Arbor University. (n.d.). *Why offer PLA?* Spring Arbor, MI.: Author.

## CHAPTER 11

Maehl, W. H. (1999). *Lifelong learning at its best: Innovative practices in adult credit programs.* Hoboken, NJ: John Wiley and Sons.

St. Edward's University. (2008). *Adult learning.* Retrieved August 23, 2008, from http://www.stedwards.edu/newc/current/services.htm

St. Edward's University. (n.d). *Portfolio advertising documents 1 & 2.* Austin, TX: Author.

St. Edward's University. (2008). *Portfolio: Frequently asked questions.* Retrieved July 29, 2008, from http://www.discoverstedwards.com/x329.xml

St. Edward's University. (n.d). *Portfolio sample: Arts Administration I.* Austin, TX: Author.

## CHAPTER 12

St. Joseph's College, School of Professional and Graduate Studies. (n.d.). *Portfolio assessment policies for evaluators.* Brooklyn, NY: Author.

St. Joseph's College, School of Professional and Graduate Studies. (n.d.). *Portfolio sample: Facilities administration.* Brooklyn, NY: Author.

St. Joseph's College, School of Professional and Graduate Studies. (n.d.). *Registration procedures and application.* Brooklyn, NY: Author.

St. Joseph's College. (n.d.) *Transfer or experiential credit.* Retrieved July 16, 2008, from http://www.sjcny.edu/printpage.php/prmID/286

St. Joseph's College. (n.d.). *Accreditations.* Retrieved July 16, 2008, from http://www.sjcny.edu/page.php/prmID/17

St. Joseph's College. (n.d.). *2007/2009 Catalogue, School of Professional and Graduate Studies.* Retrieved July 16, 2008, from http://www.sjcny.edu/media/2615_PGS CourseCatalogueBothopt.pdf

St. Joseph's College, School of Professional and Graduate Studies. (2008, Spring). *Student handbook: Portfolio and career development seminar.* Brooklyn, NY: Author.

## CHAPTER 13

Fiddler, M., Marienau, C., & Whitaker, U. (2006). *Assessing learning: Standards, principles, and procedures.* Dubuque, IA: Kendall/Hunt.

Valdosta State University. (n.d.). *Accreditation and memberships.* Retrieved July 27, 2008, from http://www.valdosta.edu/vsu/about/accreditation.shtml

Valdosta State University. (n.d.). *Application for credit through prior learning assessment (PLA): PERS 2730 Internet Technology.* Valdosta, GA: Author.

Valdosta State University. (n.d.). *Concise mission statement.* Retrieved July 27, 2008, from http://www.valdosta.edu/sra/documents/VSU_Concise_Mission.pdf

Valdosta State University. (n.d.). *Flow chart for Valdosta State University prior learning assessment (PLA) Program.* Valdosta, GA.: Author.

Valdosta State University. (n.d.). *Portfolio sample: NURS 4060 Advanced Health Assessment.* Valdosta, GA: Author.

Valdosta State University. (n.d.). *Portfolio sample: PERS 2730 Internet Technology.* Valdosta, GA: Author.

Valdosta State University. (n.d.). *Prior learning assessment (PLA) program handbook [policies and procedures for students and faculty].* Valdosta, GA: Author.

Valdosta State University. (n.d.). *Prior learning assessment resources [list of courses available via portfolio assessment].* Valdosta, GA: Author.

Valdosta State University. (n.d.). *Rubric for effective prior learning assessment submissions: NURS 4060 Advanced Health Assessment.* Valdosta, GA: Author.

Valdosta State University. (n.d.). *Rubric for effective prior learning assessment submissions: PERS 2730 Internet Technology.* Valdosta, GA: Author.

Valdosta State University. (n.d.). *The role of faculty assessors [FAQs for PLA Assessors at VSU].* Valdosta, GA: Author.

## CHAPTER 14

Community College of Vermont. (2008). *Assessment of prior learning (APL).* Retrieved August 24, 2008, from http://www.ccv.edu/apl

Vermont State Colleges. (2007, January). *Assessing experiential learning for college credit: Evaluator guidelines for assessing portfolios and awarding for experiential learning.* Montpelier, VT: Author.

Vermont State Colleges. (2006, July). *Earning college credit for prior experiential learning: A student handbook for educational assessment and portfolio preparation* (8th ed.). Montpelier, VT: Author.

Vermont State Colleges. (n.d). *Home page.* Retrieved August 9, 2008, from http://www.vsc.edu/

Vermont State Colleges. (n.d.). *Portfolio sample: Patsy Smith.* Montpelier, VT: Author.

Wikipedia. (2008, February 25). *Vermont State Colleges.* Retrieved August 9, 2008, from http://en.wikipedia.org/wiki/Vermont_State_Colleges

## CHAPTER 15

Colvin, J. (2006). *Earn college credit for what you know* (4th ed.). Chicago, IL: CAEL.

McKenzie, R. H. (1992). *Degree planning and prior learning* (3rd ed.). Dubuque, IA: Kendall/Hunt.

*Peterson's planner.* (2008). Retrieved August 3, 2008 from, http://www.petersons.com

University of Alabama External Degree Program. (n.d.). *University of Alabama Academic Programs & Services External Degree Program.* Retrieved August 3, 2008, from http://exd.ua.edu/

University of Alabama External Degree Program. (n.d.). *Portfolio sample: Management.* Tuscaloosa, AL: Author.

University of Alabama External Degree Program. (2006, December). *Prior learning student guide.* Tuscaloosa, AL: Author.

University of Alabama News Office of University Relations. (2007, December 11). *Joe Namath to receive his college degree during UA's winter commencement ceremonies Dec. 15.* Retrieved August 3, 2008, from http://uanews.ua.edu/anews2007/dec07/namath121107.htm

# INDEX

## A

AACRAO. *See* American Association of Collegiate Registrars and Admissions Officers
Academic Standards, 18
ACE. *See* American Council on Education
ACT. *See* American College Testing program
Administrative Standards, 18
admissions, open, 1–2
adult(s)
    education, history of, 59–60, 67
    experiences, expertise and talents of, 73
adult learner(s). *See also* Prior Learning Assessment
    engagement of, 13–15
    /higher education during 1970s, 1–2
    initiatives, 13
    at Spring Arbor University, 59–60
    target groups within, 13
    workshops, 7
*Adult Learning in Focus: National and State-by-State Data*, 11–12
Advanced Placement (AP), 81
    credits, 95
    Examinations, 3, 6, 103
    tools, 80
American Association of Collegiate Registrars and Admissions Officers (AACRAO), 5, 103
American College Testing program (ACT), 6, 103
American Council on Education (ACE), 5, 48, 81, 92, 103
    credits, 95, 96
    knowledge and skills assessment by, 1, 80

Office on Educational Credits and Credentials, 2, 5
    recommendations of, 25, 39
AP. *See* Advanced Placement
APCL. *See* Assessment of Prior Certificated Learning
APEL. *See* Assessment of Prior Experiential Learning
APL. *See* Assessment of prior learning
articulation, 104
Ashford University
    Capstone Course at, 26
    Center for External Studies, 25, 26
    CR-ROMs, 26–28, 31
    eligibility and access at, 26
    EXP 200 Fundamentals of Adult Learning at, 27–28
    Experiential Essay at, 27–28, 29f
    faculty compensation, 28
    fees, 28
    history, 25
    Intranet system at, 31
    mission of, 25
    PLA Credit Review Center at, 28, 30
    PLA Documentation Guide of, 26
    PLA Electronic Processing Center at, 28, 29f, 30
    PLA Information Center, 26, 28
    PLA practices at, 27–28
    PLA *Quality Assurance Model*, 26
    PLA Submission process, 29f
    portfolio assessment at, 25, 27–28
    Sponsored Professional Training at, 27–28, 29f

Ashford University (*continued*)
  statistical profile of, 31
  use of technology at, 28–31
*Assessing Learning* (CAEL), 80
*Assessing Learning: Standards, Principles & Procedures*
      (Fiddler, Marienau and Whitaker), 7
  academic standards of, 18–19
  administrative standards of, 19–20
  goals of, 17–18
  quality assurance in, 18–20
  revision of, 18
*Assessing Learning: Standards, Principles, &*
      *Procedures* (Whitaker), 6
assessment(s)
  criteria, policies and procedures of, 19
  definition of, 104
  evidence, 104, 106
  fees charged for, 20
  personnel training involved with, 20
  practices at St. Edward's University, 68–70
  principles of, 109
  programs, 20
  self-, 109
Assessment of Prior Certificated Learning (APCL),
      103
Assessment of Prior Experiential Learning (APEL),
      17, 103
Assessment of prior learning (APL). *See also* Prior
      learning assessment
  definition of, 2–3, 103
  growth of, 5–6, 17
  options, 22–24, 23*f*
  process, 21–22
  program at Vermont State Colleges, 85–90
assessor(s)
  compensation at Vermont State Colleges, 90
  definition of, 104
Athabasca University (AU)
  associated websites of, 38
  CD-ROMs, 34, 38
  Centre for Learning Accreditation at, 33, 34,
      35–36
  Course-Based Portfolio Assessment at, 34
  experiential learning at, 34
  Experimental Project for the Assessment of
      Prior Learning at, 33
  faculty compensation, 36
  fees, 36
  history, 33
  mission of, 33
  PLAR at, 34, 35, 37*f*
  portfolio assessment at, 33, 34, 35–36
  Program-Based, 34
    statistical profile of, 38
    use of technology at, 36–38
AU. *See* Athabasca University
Australia, 8

**B**

Blackboard, 26, 65, 70
Block Credit Model, 104

**C**

CAEL. *See* Council for Adult and Experiential
      Learning
Canada, 8
Carnegie Corporation, 3–4
Castleton State College, 85
certificate, 104
challenge(s)
  course, 105
  exam, 104
  of PLA, 12–15
Charter Oak State College
  assessment practices at, 42–43
  CD-ROMs, 40, 44
  establishment of, 39
  faculty compensation, 43
  fees, 43
  history, 39
  portfolio assessment at, 39
  portfolio overview at, 40
  portfolio process at, 40–42, 42*f*
  Prior Learning Portfolio Development at,
      42–43
  statistical profile of, 44
  *Student Handbook*, 40
  use of technology at, 44
CHEA. *See* Council on Higher Education
      Accreditation
CLEP. *See* College-Level Examination Program
Coalition of Lifelong Learning Organizations
      (COLLO), 105
College Board, 2
College-Level Examination Program (CLEP), 81,
      95, 105
  tests, 2, 3, 6, 25, 86
  tools, 80
college-level learning, 45, 93, 105
  definition of, 105
  student guide for, 48, 49
  workshops, 7
COLLO. *See* Coalition of Lifelong Learning
      Organizations
Commission on Colleges of the Southern
      Association of Colleges and Schools, 79

Commission on Higher Education, 73
Commission on Non-Traditional Study, 3
Community College of Vermont, 2, 4, 85–86, 87, 89
competence, 103, 107
    -based credit model, 105
    definition of, 105
    levels of, 19
Connecticut Board of Governors for Higher
    Education, 39
Contributors and Affiliations, 101–102
Council for Adult and Experiential Learning
    (CAEL), 8, 104
    Assembly, 4
    Board of Trustees, 4
    event sponsorships by, 1
    Faculty Development Program, 5
    I: assessment projects, 4
    II: publications/research/training, 4–5
    National PLA Survey, 6
    principles and standards of, 5, 86
    priorities of, 4–5
    projects, 4–5, 92
    publications by, 7–8, 80
    Steering Committee, 4
    Ten Standards for Quality Assurance, 6
    work of, 1
Council on Higher Education Accreditation
    (CHEA), 5, 104
Council on Postsecondary Education in Kentucky
    (CPE), 13
course(s)
    challenge, 105
    equivalence credit model, 105
CPE. *See* Council on Postsecondary Education
credit(s), 14, 28, 30, 48, 49, 83, 84, 105
    ACE, 2, 5, 95, 96
    AP, 95
    bank, 106
    definition of, 106
    /equivalents for learning, 18, 19
    -limits for PLA at University of Alabama
        External Degree Program, 94–95
    transfer, 110
*Creditable Portfolios: Dimensions in Diversity,* 5
criteria(s)
    assessment policies, procedures and, 19
    definition of, 106

**D**

DANTES. *See* Defense Activity for Non-Traditional
    Educational Support
DANTES Subject Standard Tests (DSST), 3, 25, 95,
    106

Defense Activity for Non-Traditional Educational
    Support (DANTES), 80–81, 106
DePaul University, 7–8
distance education, 106
DSST. *See* DANTES Subject Standard Tests
Dunham, Alden, 4

**E**

*Earn College Credit for What You Know* (Simosko,
    Lamdin, Colvin), 5, 7
education
    adult, 59–60, 67
    distance, 106
    distributed, 106
    higher, 1–2
    history of adult, 59–60, 67
    intermittent enrollment and, 1–2
    non-traditional, 3
Educational Foundation of America, 3
Educational Testing Service (ETS), 3
El Paso Community College, 3
Empire State College (New York), 2, 3
    assessment practices at, 48–51, 50*f*
    associated websites of, 52
    CD-ROMs at, 47, 49, 52
    Center for Distance Learning, 51
    Center Office of Academic Review at, 46–47,
        48–51, 50*f*
    establishment of, 45
    experiential learning at, 46–48
    history, 45
    Office of College-wide Academic Review at, 49
    PLA programs at, 46
    portfolio assessment at, 45–46
    statistical profile of, 52
    *A Student Guide: Credit for Prior College-level
        Learning and Student Degree Planning Guide,*
        48, 49
    use of technology at, 51
England, 8
Erkennen Vanelders of Informed Verworven
    Competencies (EVC), 103, 107
ETS. *See* Educational Testing Service
evaluation, 107
Evans, Norman, 8
EVC. *See* Erkennen Vanelders of Informed
    Verworven Competencies
evidence of learning, 104, 106
exam(s). *See also* College-Level Examination
    Program
    AP, 3, 6, 103
    challenge, 104
    college, 3
    Excelsior, 3, 25, 95

Excelsior exams, 3, 25, 95
EXD. *See* University of Alabama External Degree
      Program
experience(s)
    adults' expertise, talents and, 73
    learning, 17, 93, 98–99, 107
*Experiential Learning Around the World* (Evans), 8

## F

feedback, 107
Figures, 23,  29, 30, 37, 41, 50, 54, 63, 76, 82
Florida International University, 2, 3
Framingham State College, 3
France, 8

## G

GED (General Education Diploma), 13
General Education Diploma. *See* GED
Georgia, 79
goal statement, 107

## H

higher education
    /adult learners during 1970s, 1–2
    pressures on, 2

## I

IAP. *See* individual academic plans
IDP. *See* Institutional Development Program
individual academic plans (IAP), 60
Institutional Development Program (IDP), 55
Intranet system, at Ashford University, 31
Ireland, 8
iWebfolio software, 70

## J

Johnson State College, 85

## K

Keeton, Morris, 4–5
Kentucky
    Adult Learner Initiative, 13
    CPE, 13
    PLA in, 12–13
    target groups in, 13

## L

learners, adult. *See* adult learners
learning, 19. *See also* Prior Learning Assessment
    assessment of, 18–20
    college-level, 7, 45, 48, 49, 93, 105
    credits or equivalents for, 18, 19

distance, 106
evidence of, 104, 105
experiences, 17, 93, 98–99, 107
experiential, 5, 34, 45, 46–48, 74–75, 76, 107
extra-institutional, 14
level of acceptable, 19
lifelong, 107
measurement of, 108
nonformal, 108
nonsponsored, 108
open, 108
outcome, 107
prior, 2
processes, 19
self-directed, 109
sponsored, 109
standards for assessment of, 17–20
transcripts and, 19
letter of testimony, 107
Lyndon State College, 85

## M

Maryhill College, 67
mentoring, 108
Metropolitan State University. *See* Minnesota
    Metropolitan State College
Meyer, Jean, 67
Michigan, 49, 64
Michigan Fire Fighter's Training Council, 64
Microsoft, 56, 65, 83
Middle States Association of Colleges and Schools,
    73
Minnesota
    Higher Education Fairness Statute, 13
    PLA in, 12, 13–14
Minnesota Department of Employment and
    Economic Development, 13
Minnesota Metropolitan State College, 2, 3
Minnesota National Guard, 13
Minnesota State Colleges and Universities
    (MnSCU), 13–14
Minnesota State Legislature, 12, 13–14
MnSCU. *See* Minnesota State Colleges and
    Universities

## N

National Program on Non-collegiate Sponsored
    Instruction (NPONSI), 48
*New Directions for Experiential Learning*
    (Jossey-Bass), 5
New England Association of Schools and Colleges,
    39

New York State Education Department, 73
New Zealand, 8
"non-traditional programs," 2
NPONSI. *See* National Program on Non-collegiate Sponsored Instruction

**O**
Ohio, 49
Oklahoma
  PLA in, 12, 14
  *Reach Higher* program in, 14
Oklahoma State Regents for Higher Education, 14
Open Learning Agency, 107

**P**
Pennsylvania
  *Job Ready*, 15
  PLA in, 12, 15
Pennsylvania Department of Education, 15
Pennsylvania Department of Labor and Industry, 15
Pennsylvania State Board of Education, 15
Peruniak, Geoff, 33
PLA. *See* Prior Learning Assessment
PLAR. *See* Prior Learning Assessment and Recognition
PONSI, 25, 39
portfolio(s). *See also* Prior Learning Assessment
  definition of, 108
  development, 108
  for evaluation, 22
  evaluators at St. Edward's University, 70
  fees, 56
  grading, 55–56
  overview at Charter Oak State College, 40
  overview at Regis University, 55
  PLA Advising & Administrative Guidance, 23
  PLA processes, 22–24
  PLA programs, 3, 5–6
  process at Charter Oak State College, 40–42, 42*f*
  process at Vermont State Colleges, 89
  sample at Vermont State Colleges, 88–89
  student, 7, 22–24, 77, 88–89
  transcripts at Vermont State Colleges, 89
portfolio assessment, 5
  at Ashford University, 25, 27–28
  at Athabasca University, 33, 34, 35–36
  at Charter Oak State College, 39
  at Empire State College (New York), 45–46
  at Regis University, 55
  use of, 6
prerequisite, 109

*Principles of Good Practice in Assessing Experiential Learning* (Willingham), 6
Prior Learning Assessment (PLA). *See also* Assessment of prior learning; *specific colleges and universities*
  *101,* 7
  during the 1980s, 5–6
  abroad, 8
  acceptance of, 5, 17
  accessibility to, 12
  *Advising Adult Learners* workshops by, 7
  Advising and Administrative Guidance, 22, 23*f*
  affordability of, 12
  approaches to, 3
  aspirations of, 12
  Certificate of Professional Achievement workshop, 8
  Certification Program, 7–8
  challenges of, 12–15
  conclusions on, 15–16
  *Defining College-Level Learning* workshops by, 7
  definition of, 2–3, 103, 108
  extra credits through, 14
  history of, 1
  introduction to, 11–12
  in Kentucky, 12–13
  methods/practices, 6, 15–16
  in Minnesota, 12, 13–14
  national surveys on, 6, 7*f*
  in Oklahoma, 12, 14
  opportunities, 21–22, 23*f*
  in Pennsylvania, 12, 15
  philosophical basis of, 1
  policies of, 15–16
  portfolio processes within, 22–24
  portfolio programs in, 3, 5–6
  progress of, 8
  resources and training opportunities within, 7–8
  states involved with, 12–16
  students' choices regarding, 21–22
  thirty years of, 1–10
  timeline of, 9–10
  workshops, 7–8
*Prior Learning Assessment: A Guidebook to American Institutional Practices* (Flint, Johnson, Zucker), 6
Prior Learning Assessment and Recognition (PLAR), 17, 103, 108
  at Athabasca University, 34, 35, 37*f*

*Prior Learning Assessment at Home and Abroad,* 6
*Prior Learning Assessment: Results of a Nationwide Institutional Survey* (Chapman and Fugate), 6
"Prior Learning Portfolios: A Representative Collection," 7
*A Prior Learning Assessment and Recognition (PLAR) at Athabasca University: A Handbook for Preparing Portfolios,* 34, 36

## Q
quality assurance, 26
 in *Assessing Learning: Standards, Principles & Procedures,* 18–20
 CAEL's Ten Standards for, 6
 definition of, 109

## R
RDA. *See* Reconnaissance des Acquis
Recognition of Prior Learning (RPL), 103, 109
Reconnaissance des Acquis (RDA), 103, 109
References, 111–117
Regis College, 53
Regis University
 CD-ROMs at, 57
 College for Professional Studies at, 53
 establishment of, 53
 PLA at, 53–55, 54f
 PLA eligibility at, 55
 PLA practices at, 53–55, 54f
 portfolio overview at, 55
 Rueckert-Hartman College for Health Professions at, 53
 statistical profile of, 57
 use of technology at, 56
Rendell, Edward G., 15
residency requirement, 109
Roman Catholic Congregation of Holy Cross (Austin, Texas), 67
RPL. *See* Recognition of Prior Learning
Rydell, Susan, 5

## S
St. Edward's University
 assessment practices at, 68–70
 CD-ROMs, 69, 71
 Center for Prior Learning Assessment, 68
 contract faculty at, 70
 eligibility and access at, 68
 establishment of, 67
 New College, 67–71
 PLA at, 68

 portfolio evaluators at, 70
 Prior Learning Assessment Seminar, 68–70
 statistical profile of, 70–71
 use of technology at, 70
St. Joseph's College
 assessment practices of, 75, 76f
 CD-ROMs, 74–75, 78
 establishment of, 73
 faculty compensation, 75
 fees, 75
 PLA at, 73–75, 76f
 Prior Experiential Learning Assessment Program at, 74–75, 76
 School of Professional and Graduate Studies, 73–74
 statistical profile of, 78
 *Student Handbook 2007/2008,* 75, 76
 student portfolio petitions at, 77
 use of technology at, 77
San Francisco State College, 3
San Francisco State University. *See* San Francisco State College
Scotland, 8
self-assessment, 109
self-directed learning, 109
Sinclair Community College, 21
skill(s)
 ACE's assessment of knowledge and, 1, 80
 -set, 109
 transferable, 110
South Africa, 8
Southern Association of Colleges and Schools (SACS), 79, 92
Spring Arbor University
 "Adult Development and Life Planning" class at, 60
 assessment practices at, 62
 CD-ROMs, 60–61, 62, 66
 "Center Assessment and Planning" module at, 60
 establishment of, 59
 faculty, 62–64
 fees at, 64–65
 history of adult education at, 59–60
 Life-Learning Papers at, 60–61, 62–65, 63f
 PLA at, 60–65, 63f
 PLA limitations and requirements at, 62
 Professional Schools and Training at, 60–61
 School of Adult Studies, 59–60
 statistical profile of, 65–66
 student preparations at, 62
 use of technology at, 65

*A Student Guide: Credit for Prior College-level Learning and Student Degree Planning Guide* (Empire State College), 48, 49
student(s)
    choices regarding PLA, 21–22
    portfolio petitions at St. Joseph's College, 77
    portfolios, 7, 22–24, 77, 88–89
    preparations at Spring Arbor University, 62

**T**

Tate, Pamela, 5
TECEP, 25
technology
    Ashford University's use of, 28–31
    Athabasca University's use of, 36–38
    Charter Oak State College's use of, 44
    Empire State College's use of, 51
    Regis University's use of, 56
    St. Edward's University's use of, 70
    St. Joseph's College's use of, 77
    Spring Arbor University's use of, 65
    Valdosta State University's at, 83
    Vermont State Colleges' use of, 90
Terms and Abbreviations, 1–3, 110
Thomas A. Edison State College (New Jersey), 2, 3
transcript(s), 110
    learning, 19
    Vermont State Colleges, 89
transfer credit, 110
transferable skills, 110

**U**

United States, 8, 11
United States Armed Services Institute, 2
University of Alabama, 3
    New College, 2, 3
University of Alabama External Degree Program (EXD)
    CD-ROMs, 95, 96, 99
    credit-limits for PLA at, 94–95
    currency of knowledge at, 97
    decision appeals at, 96–97
    establishment of, 91
    fees at, 96
    mission and purpose of, 91–92
    modified ASK at, 96, 97, 98–99
    modified portfolios at, 98–99
    Office of Public Relations at, 91
    parts of portfolio at, 95–96
    PLA at, 92
    PLA portfolio at, 93–94
    portfolio preparation at, 94

    portfolio process at, 97–98
    portfolio transcripts at, 96
    *Prior Learning Student Guide,* 95
    rationale for PLA at, 92–93
    regular ASK at, 95–96, 97
    statistical profile of, 99
    time-limits for assessment of portfolio at, 94
    timetable for portfolio at, 94
    transferability of prior learning credits at, 96
University of Massachusetts at Boston College of Public and Community Service, 2

**V**

Valdosta State University
    Application for Credit Through Prior Learning Assessment, 83, 84
    associated websites of, 84
    CD-ROMs, 80–81, 83, 84
    direction and support established at, 80–81
    eligibility and access at, 81, 82*f*
    faculty at, 80–81
    history, 79
    mission of, 79
    PLA at, 79–83, 82*f*
    PLA Pilot Project, 79–80, 83
    statistical profile of, 84
    Student Success Center at, 81
    use of technology at, 83
Vermont General Assembly, 85
Vermont State Colleges
    APL program at, 85–90
    assessment practices at, 88
    assessor compensation at, 90
    CD-ROMs, 87, 90
    enrollment at, 87
    establishment of, 85
    fees, 90
    Interactive Television Network, 87
    Office of External Programs, 85–86, 89
    portfolio process at, 89
    portfolio sample at, 88–89
    portfolio transcripts at, 89
    statistical profile at, 90
    use of technology at, 90
    websites associated with, 87
Vermont Technical College, 85

**W**

WebCT Vista software, 83
Whitaker, Urban, 6
W.K. Kellogg Foundation, 5
World War II, 1